MW01133044

Mindfulness
and Surfing

Mindfulness
and Surfing

Reflections for Saltwater Souls

Sam Bleakley

Leaping Hare Press

This edition published in the UK and North America in 2017 by

Leaping Hare Press

An imprint of The Quarto Group
The Old Brewery, 6 Blundell Street
London N7 9BH, United Kingdom
T (0)20 7700 6700 **F** (0)20 7700 8066
www.Quarto.com

First published in the UK in 2016

Text © 2016 Sam Bleakley
Design and layout © 2017 Quarto Publishing plc

British Library Cataloguing-in-Publication Data
A catalogue record for this book is available from
the British Library

ISBN: 978-1-78240-329-6

This book was conceived, designed and produced by

Leaping Hare Press

Publisher SUSAN KELLY
Creative Director MICHAEL WHITEHEAD
Editorial Director TOM KITCH
Commissioning Editor MONICA PERDONI
Art Director WAYNE BLADES
Project Editors JAYNE ANSELL, JOANNA BENTLEY
Editor JENNI DAVIS
Designer GINNY ZEAL
Illustrator MELVYN EVANS

Printed in Singapore

9 10

CONTENTS

CHAPTER ONE

TAKING OFF

*Every surfer craves the experience of surfing
with dolphins, or sitting close to basking sharks
in blue-green water. I have surfed with dolphins,
seals, sharks and sea snakes. I have sensed the sudden
suspension of time — sought by all meditative
techniques — deep inside the 'tube'; and been clipped
by that same wave, then dragged across a razor-sharp
live coral reef as the water curtain falls to the sea god's
applause. I have nearly drowned at the hands of
powerful waves and saved another from drowning.
And I have seen suffering men and women
reborn and healed through surfing.*

OCEAN HEALING

When I take off on a wave, poised on a sliver of surfboard, I am both fish and bird. On each occasion of bliss and fear, I am educated into the complex ways of the sea — a constant lesson in mindfulness.

MINDFULNESS IS USUALLY DESCRIBED as an inward-looking process of stopping, reflecting and clearing the mind in learning a discipline of meditation or Zen awareness. Among the hustle and bustle of contemporary life, moments of stillness can help us to regain a sense of self, of composure or centring. Mindfulness has also been used widely to combat anxiety and depression.

Surfing as mindfulness, however, does something a little different. It does not simply take us inside ourselves to find a still centre, but rather orients us within the environment to find place. We are immersed in water and the salt-soaked zone just above the sea's skin. Around us, terns dive and fish jump. We are active, alert and intent on balance. Mindfulness in surfing is then, paradoxically, a moving out of mind into the world, moving against the grain of inner-directed thought and reflection into an acute sense of what the environment demands of us — where winds, currents, beach shapes, wave types and lunar-tidal movements meet. In this sense, we move from 'egology' to ecology and we generate a 'bodymindfulness', locating ourselves in place and space.

From Ego to Eco

For over two thousand years the Western world has developed techniques of focus on the self and the inward life. The invention of autobiography as a literary genre in the eighteenth century and its perfection in personal-confessional styles across all media – such as kiss-and-tell journalism, selfies or *YouTube* videos – has, arguably, dried up our receptivity to the outer world as we become acutely sensitive to the inner life. As a result, we have an egological surplus and an ecological crisis. We need to recover sensitivity towards the world around us – its cries and pleasures, its sufferings and beauties. Surfing is an ideal way to do this as a mindfulness given by nature. The saltwater soul of surfing is to be mindful of nature's body as we cultivate a 'bodymind'.

As a novice, you will spend far more time spilled into the sea than standing on your board surfing a wave, and so the apprenticeship into an ecological perception, or being mindful of nature's body, can be tough and uncomfortable – especially in cold seas and even in state-of-the-art wetsuits. But as you gain expertise so you will gradually gain a more graceful, elegant and inventive approach to how you relate to waves – in other words, you will develop a mindfulness in the ocean. It is the ocean and not surfing instructors that will teach you this mindfulness, and to which you must adapt. As expertise develops, the surfer becomes a connoisseur of the oceans, tutored and formed by them.

Outside-In

The psychologist James Gibson (1904–79) revolutionized the way we think about perception in his model of 'ecological perception'. In Gibson's view, the world is not passively received by the senses and then processed cognitively via the brain and central nervous system – this is an inside-out perspective. Rather, the world actively educates our attention to its shapes, patterns, motions, colours, smells, tastes, vibrations, rhythms, oscillations and (dis)appearances. The world captures our attention, shaping and dictating what and how we sense. Further, the senses do not act independently but in concert as a sensorium or a total system, again shaped by environmental 'affordances', as Gibson described them – patterns of attraction that draw us to them and make us *notice*.

Educated by the Ocean

The sea and its waves, formed by storms in deep water and fetched along miles of open ocean to unfold on reefs and coasts, are largely untouched by human culture in its energies and forms, even if there is pollution and rising sea levels through global warming. Pitching back in to the natural world of the ocean and its patterns moves us closer to an ecological perception without the filter of cultural perception. Surfing brings you face to face with the raw beauty of nature at different volumes and tones, and in this setting there is the opportunity to be mindful not by moving inwards to the self but by adapting to what the environment affords. The ozone-filled environment, the salt-stained bath, the imminent contact with sea life, the swell of the waves – all of this places the surfer, beginner, intermediate or expert, into a mindfulness relationship with the environment as an ecological rather than egological activity. As one is taught and shaped by the ocean – its waves, currents, tides, sea life, colours, temperatures, forms and patterns – so one becomes more tuned to its needs and then more ecologically minded and sensitive. As

Surfing brings you face to face with the raw beauty of nature

the elegance, determination, skill and courage of the surfer grow, so s/he becomes more environmentally aware as a form of 'external' mindfulness.

I hope this book will guide you through the anatomy of a mindfulness of surfing through which an acute ecological perception is recovered. The minds of people do not need to be tuned to their own needs and purposes as much as to the needs and purposes of the environments in which they live, for it is these environments that sustain us. Caring for our oceans and coastlines is part of this perceptual tuning and action. And surfing is a great vehicle for getting us right into the heart of the oceans' and coastlines' workings so that they can teach us how to care for them, and above all, how to be mindful. Enjoy the ride!

THE WATER CURTAIN
FALLS TO A GOD'S APPLAUSE

◆

The wave feathers and breaks over the shallow coral reef, a falling curtain of water. I am moving fast across the face, angled, alert. Time seems to slow and expand in the eerie silence. Surfing at these moments acutely awakens the senses and touches the ineffable.

T HE 'TUBE' IS THE ULTIMATE DESTINATION for every surfer – standing on the surfboard behind the falling curtain of water as if at the back of a waterfall, trying to stay ahead of its collapse. Surfing and life can be defined as how well you can stay in balance as all around you cascades, or, as surfers put it, 'clocking up tube time' – being in the most critical part of the wave for as long as possible. But when the curtain falls and you are deep in the tuberide, you may not make the exit, and sharp, infectious coral might rake, brand and scar your back with unwanted tattoos straight from nature's hand as you 'wipeout', or fall off the board. Water's motion is the flux of the Tao (which simply means 'the Way') – the forgiving yin against the fearless yang. 'Highest good is like water,' wrote the Chinese philosopher Lao Tzu. 'It comes close to the Way.'

A current estimate for the global surfing population is 30 million people. Surfing is largely focused on the sea but there is lake surfing (winds, for example, create surfable waves on the Great Lakes straddling North America and even the

Caspian Sea coast of Azerbaijan), river surfing (along periodic tidal bores like the 'Silver Dragon' on the Qiantang in China) and a growing interest in developing inland wave gardens, which I discuss in the final chapter. If you think about the coastline of any sea-kissed country, it is generally indented because of the action of waves and tides. Pull that coastline out straight and you have an enormous mileage, inviting surfers. The growing surfing culture is also diverse, exhibiting a significant shift in demographics, including a broadening age range, increasing participation of women, multi-ethnic and multi-ability backgrounds and vulnerable members of society. Surfing is used therapeutically, too, for example to treat post-traumatic stress disorder and to channel the energies of otherwise wild kids. One of the top women professional surfers, Bethany Hamilton, lost an arm in a shark attack, yet still surfs at the highest level.

Surfers as Activists

In my own backyard, wherever the turbulent Atlantic greets the UK's rugged coastline, sometimes with a kiss, mostly with a slap, there is now a thriving surf culture – an estimated 500,000 souls becoming aware of the delicate balance between the natural setting of sea life and human cultural impact. Some of those surfers are proud political activists. No surfer wants to paddle out in polluted waters, or sit back without protest while a pristine stretch of coast is 'developed'

as a marina. It was surfers who first noticed how much raw sewage floated around the UK's coastline and protested.

In 1990, the environmental action group Surfers Against Sewage (SAS) was formed in Cornwall. Following ten years of campaigning, private water companies finally started to invest in comprehensive sewage treatment schemes, and today SAS can be proud of the number of the UK's Blue Flags – a European-wide strategy that rewards clean bathing waters.

I am a keen member of SAS. But I am also of the generation that has been brought up on acquisition and uncritical adoption of the latest 'must-have' technologies and gadgetry. The surfboard industry has a toxic past, heavily reliant on oil-based chemicals grafted from the aerospace industry in the 1950s. Polyurethane foam and fibreglass, although carcinogenic, was cheap, versatile, had a cosmetic appeal, tolerated thermal ranges and was easy to construct, giving rise to constantly evolving surfboard designs. Eventually, the leading American manufacturer of foam was closed down because the product had broken the relatively lax environmental laws. The reaction has been a new wave of small-scale, ecologically sensitive production – reflecting the Polynesian roots of wave-riding when Hawaiians carved select redwood trees. In this reflexive move to be accountable to the environment for the surfboards you ride, surfers are fast becoming green ambassadors.

Surfers are fast becoming green ambassadors

Call of the Wild

Surfing becomes addictive and you follow, but it is probably better to think of this as a calling, a vocation – Jack London's 'call of the wild' translated from the Yukon to any surfable coastline. As a professional surfer who also makes a living from travel writing, I have followed the pursuit around the world and clocked up many guilty air miles. It is common to see beaches openly used as dumps and toilets, littered with plastics. But there is always choice and, paradoxically, it is long-term contact with the ocean that will force us into unavoidable choices, for the deterioration of the marine environment is happening at a rate that must be curtailed. We are all familiar with the news of species depletion by overfishing, of the death of coral beds and the problems of oil spills, microplastics and sewage pollution. What is not so widely broadcast is, for example, the increasing amount of medical waste deposited from ships.

The potential ecological awareness of surfers – a kind of megabody of sensitivity to the environment – offers a powerful collective imagery – caring for the environment. But how

◆

The water, like witch's oils

Burnt green, and blue, and white.

FROM 'THE RIME OF THE ANCIENT MARINER'
SAMUEL TAYLOR COLERIDGE, ENGLISH POET AND PHILOSOPHER, 1772–1834

◆

do we harness this holistic knowing of the nature and beauty of the sea to transform it into action for collective good as an ecological imperative? Most surfers are naturally Friends of the Ocean – they are already badged, stained by salt residues. But, as ever, there are contradictions at work. Some surfing communities are infamous for their aggressive localism, protecting 'their' local break from visitors. This is plain nonsense – no group of people 'owns' the ocean in this way, and surfers must face this fact.

The world works on us, or 'affords' us perception, and we respond to its lessons. The world is a gift, not a commodity. If we were to take on this idea, then we would not be so eager to shape the world to our desires, but rather to appreciate how the world educates us into her presence and beauty. The admirable surfers, out of the loop of localism and unnecessary aggressive mentality, allow the wave to shape their responses rather than impose themselves on the wave. As the poet Wallace Stevens (1879–1955) wrote, 'The world is presence, not force.' The world does not set out to control us, it merely presents itself in all its glory and moods, yet we are bent on controlling it and our methods have been crude, destructive and are now boomeranging back with a vengeance.

The world is a gift, not a commodity

Surfing as Meditation

Surfing immediately facilitates immersion in the present. The very act of engaging with surfing educates acute sensitivity to coastlines, location and movement. The dance of surfing is an embodied performance that frequently touches upon spiritual experience where time slews in the strangest of ways.

The saying 'If you see the Buddha on the road, kill him' means that one does not worship or idolize the figure of the Buddha, the Buddha as personality or, these days, as celebrity. Rather, you follow the Way of the Buddha precisely by demolishing his image and creating fresh perspective. Buddhism is not carried by a figure but by the wisdom of the teaching only revealed by the 'murder' of the teacher. Similarly, if you think that surfing will automatically translate into a mindful activity, you have not yet killed surfing. To 'perform' surfing is a first step, to 'think with' surfing is a second step, to let surfing think you and perform you, or to be shaped by the total environment that we conveniently reduce to the act of 'surfing', is a more expansive step still. There is no better way to let surfing think you than to go surfing armed with what I will call a 'reflexive instinct', an animal knowing that is 'knowing in the bodymind' – explored and explained throughout this book, perhaps taking the notion of 'mindfulness' a step further.

MINDFULNESS EXERCISE

SEA AIR SOUND THERAPY

In the Cornish language, there is a word for the ever-present, grinding, moaning sound of the sea – *mordros*. Set against this background drive is the single feathering wave – *mordon* – which is a feminine word. The wave rises, light and crisp, breaking free from the anchor that is the deep swell, the incessant tidal motion, the undercurrent, the pulse. Waves are a delicate *presence* woven into the sea's *force*. To meet this graceful presence, surfers will need poise.

This exercise is about listening to the interaction of elements at the coast (tide, wind and wave), best experienced when the wind is onshore (blowing from sea to land).

Find a safe lookout spot where you can both see the ocean and feel the wind. The texture of the surf changes dramatically depending on the wind direction: an onshore wind will create 'white heads' and what surfers call 'chop'; an offshore wind will smooth out the uneven texture creating 'clean conditions'. The wind will produce sound, but so will the sea – quite simply, the bigger the waves, the louder the crashing noise. The original source of every wave is the friction of wind blowing across the sea surface, therefore the onshore wind sustains a particular relationship with waves that bring this mindfulness exercise to life.

Either sitting or standing, with the kiss of the wind on your face and the waves in sight, close your eyes. Breathe slowly, with a steady cycle, in through your nose, with a depth that allows you to hear the air in the back of your throat. Visualize a horizon across your eyes. Follow this line from its centre, moving away towards your ears. Tune in to the sound of the sea. Let the waves, tide and wind merge as one. Now your breathing can begin to mirror the rhythm of this sound. The trick at this point is to not be sucked in to your inner world, but to stay focused on the sounds, smells and tastes of the environment and allow them to shape your experience. 'Bodymindful-ness' is not being in your mind, but being present in the environment.

Open your palms and further feel this wind and wave-borne sound. Fill every breath with the sound scale of waves. Let it wash over every sense and open your eyes filled with the moment. Sustain that sense of sound and use it to stay stimulated for your surf, or perhaps your swim. Imagine this as a kind of rinsing of your senses. This 'close noticing' will bring you even closer to body and spirit. If you are lucky enough to be able to paddle out into that cauldron of water, this exercise should wash out any sense of frustration about the conditions on offer, and perhaps improve your awareness of where the waves are breaking and ringing out their loudest melody. Have a walk along the tideline before you enter the water. Once you have done this exercise a few times, you can translate it into a visualization for the office. Visualize yourself at the coastline, sounds rushing through, and merge with the body of the weather.

Summary
Listen closely to the sound of the sea. Resist going into your mind. Stick with the senses as they are shaped by the sea's sound, taste and smell. Bathe in the rainbows that peel off the back of waves combed by offshore winds. Emerge refreshed.

THE STORY OF THE STRINGER

◆

To 'go surfing' is to be absorbed in the history of the activity and in its cultural and artistic meanings. Central to the form and function of the surfboard is the stringer. It runs the length of a surfboard and gives it strength.

T HE STRINGER WAS CONCEIVED in California in the late 1950s as a way to remove flex from polyurethane foam surfboard cores (known as 'blanks') and thus add strength. A breaking wave can offer a powerful punch, often slapping down on a board, and while hardened fibreglass and resin provides a waterproof casing for polyurethane foam blanks, the whole structure is actually vulnerable and can snap easily. In the transition from heavier wooden boards of the 1940s to foam and fibreglass boards in the 1950s, what was needed was a backbone, and what better way to maintain tradition than to make that backbone out of the wooden body of the original boards of Hawaii (the ancient home of surfing), to maintain a guiding myth in material form such as a thin strip of redwood or balsa. Surfboard builders (known as 'shapers') and surfers will say that it is choice of stringer that gives the board strength and character.

As soon as a backbone was introduced, an aesthetic evolved in surfboard design, and a board took on perfect symmetry. Where the blank is sawn in half from nose (front) to tail and then the two sides are glued on to the wood stringer, the stringer becomes the axis around which a board is shaped. Just as the differing kinds of wood of the ancient Hawaiian boards had symbolic meaning, so the stringer is a code referencing the origins of surfing, a residue, a memory recreated every time that a board is ridden.

Ghosts of Hawaiian Royalty

I got my first connection to Hawaiian surfing not via a trip to the Pacific, or an ancient Hawaiian wooden board itself, but through a humble British-built 1960s board with a balsa stringer as wide as two thumbs that took my imagination right back to the very roots of wave-riding. When I rode that board, ghosts of Hawaiian royalty seemed to come in and out of focus in the glassy water, cheering me on.

It was 1990 and a friend of my dad was getting rid of an old board that had been knocking around a barn for over twenty years. We got the address and called in to a farmhouse just outside Penzance, Cornwall. It was up high on the moors with views across to St Michael's Mount. The moors harboured the remains of Neolithic graveyards, Bronze Age stone circles, Iron Age settlements, and the first post-industrial landscape with the now derelict tin mines – fenced-off shafts and crumbling engine houses. This land (where I had grown up) was for me both the end of the earth and the beginning of the world, one moment bathed in reflected light from

the ocean, the next, stark, sinister and bleak as a slate-grey storm moved up the foot and ankle of the UK like a giant rolling up a sock.

The board was in the corner of a cattle shed lined with cobwebs and packed with musty, pale hay bales, readily blending in – it was mud brown. It looked like a burden rather than a treasure, and certainly not as elaborate as the weather changes we were experiencing as the rain began to strike like a drum roll on the barn roof.

'It was apparently built in 1965,' said the owner. 'Nine feet six inches long Bilbo, shaped by Cornishman Bill Bailey.'

'It's an antique,' said my dad. 'Bill Bailey was one of the first surfboard shapers in Europe.' Dad too was an antique – 1965 was the year he started surfing, in Newquay, at age fifteen, also on a Bill Bailey shaped board. My jaw fell.

The rain had eased and we strapped the Bilbo to the roof rack and headed straight home. Just around the corner from Land's End above Gwenver beach cliffs, I laid the board on the kitchen table, applied some wax (for traction) and suddenly it started to become a thing of beauty, elegantly curved at the front and back with a big fin. Mud brown became golden brown. Burden became treasure. I hauled it down the cliff path on my own at Gwenver as a thick mist rolled in.

It was extremely heavy to carry, but once in the water its weight seemed to evaporate. Surfing it began with watching the ocean and making sense of the conditions so that I could use the rip currents to paddle out (where the waves do not break, making paddling easier). The sky now hung like a dripping cloth and the mist enveloped me. First wave: wipeout. After several failed efforts, I became conscious that the wide stringer acted like landing lights for a plane or cats' eyes on a road – vital in the mist. Next wave I rode at a clean angle in perfect trim. Suddenly the board flew like an angel. It cut through the wave surface smoothly, hugging the water, in contrast to the small and lightweight shortboards I was used to, which could be jerky and awkward because they were loose and unstable. This apparently beastly board demanded elegant surfing.

Walking the Board

Shortboards (developed first in Australia in the late 1960s) are thinner and lighter than longboards (around 2.75 m or 9 ft long) and are ridden to get maximum speed and manoeuvrability. Longboards – the original Hawaiian and Californian boards, considered defunct following the late 1960s shortboard revolution – were reintroduced into surfing in the '80s and '90s. They allow more glide on a wave and, because of the length, can be 'walked'. Where you stand in one place on a shortboard, a longboard allows you to adjust weight ('trimming') to get the best speed from the critical part of the wave by changing stance in a time-honoured tradition – 'walking' the board by cross-stepping up to the nose (front) and back.

The elegance and cat-like agility of cross-stepping marks out the best longboard surfers, who are essentially dancers.

That wooden stringer was the middle road that I briefly eyed as I rode and trimmed along. Just standing in one place and gliding across a body of water is, of course, a thrill. But in order to maintain speed and respond to the curving, sometimes twisting, often flattening, occasionally steepening nature of a breaking wave, you have to change position on the board. There is a strict style convention that 'walking' the board means cross-stepping – gracefully putting one foot over the other. It came naturally to me, instinctively, because it is the most functional way to move up and down the board (just like walking a tightrope). A longboarding 'no-no' is to shuffle up and down the board, or move without cross-stepping. This is considered ugly and lazy, an insult to the shaper and to Huey, the surf god known to all old-timers.

Ten Toes Over

I was soon riding the old Bilbo as a big autumn swell was marching into Gwenver. My confidence was ripe. I easily got into position for the first wave in the next set. I pulled up a high line, walked gingerly to the nose – one step, two steps, three steps – and rolled five toes over the nose of the board. The moment they curled around the tip, I experienced a blaze of energy. I matched it with a soul arch, strong at the hips but arching my back, thus taking a little weight off the tip of the board, allowing for a longer noseride. It was a classic posture that 1960s longboarder David Nuuhiwa employed – I had studied it on surf videos.

Then I stepped forward and hung ten (all ten toes curled around the nose). I felt like I had tapped a hidden source. The long fin was so locked into the wave I threw a second soul arch before walking back. I could hear hoots from the crowd behind. They were convinced. The biggest surfwear company of the 1960s, Hang Ten, showed two bare feet as its trademark, and it became a symbol of surfing. Thirty years later, I realized that all surfers still knew the semiotics – ten toes over. It still raised a cheer of respect.

Longboarding became my passion and my career as a professional on a circuit of contests. I won the Cornish, English, British and then European Longboard Championships and surfed in the World Longboard Championships many times. Longboard surfing has consumed me. As a Geography graduate from Cambridge University, I melded my passion for surfing with a passion for travel, writing and understanding cultures, often in previously unsurfed places such as Mauritania, Haiti and China. Along the way I have developed a heartfelt appreciation of the relationship between surfing and mindfulness. I hope I can share some of this so others can also enjoy the ocean, surfing and surf travel in a safe, spirited, ethical and positive way.

> *I felt like I had tapped a hidden source*

CHAPTER TWO

OCEAN SWELL

*Throw a stone into a pond
and ripples spread as the stone displaces the
water. Imagine the stone as a tight concentration of
low pressure, a wild wind that presses down heavy on
the surface of the water, far out in the middle of the
ocean. This depression — a storm — causes giant ripples
to move out concentrically, marching across the ocean
to deposit themselves along coastlines. Where the
travelling deep-water waves suddenly strike a shallow
rock or sand bottom, they rear up like a frightened
horse, forming a 'curl' — the natural home for
surfboard and surfer.*

LIQUID LANDSCAPE

◆

A curl, the liquid living room that a wave makes as it folds over, is the space that surfers crave to inhabit. And the surfer's travelling furniture – the surfboard – is made to best inhabit this fast-moving, majestic blue-green room.

WHEN COMBED BY AN OFFSHORE WIND (blowing from land to sea), waves take on a perfect arc with a polished wall (called 'the face') and an open jaw. A surfboard locks on to the face and glides at maximum speed across the curl, caressing it, in what surfers call 'perfect trim'. Surfboards are also made to 'carve' the face, to angle across the curl, slicing the wave like a cake.

As the wave breaks, under the right conditions, one of the biggest challenges and rewards is to slot into the curl as the wave folds over you without getting knocked off by the crashing whitewater. Inside the tube – 'the green room' – for seconds only, time seems to slow, and there is an eerie feeling of being suspended. It is a feeling surfers crave, permanently. Relatively few get to sense the tuberide or the hang ten, yet all surfing in some way revolves around these possibilities – first of fitting into the curl, and hopefully of the curl developing into a tuberide, or pushing the back of the board down just enough so that you can balance at the other end, like a seesaw, literally a sea-saw – and your heart leaps.

Threefold Way

A moving hump of glaucous green water races towards me as I sit astride a longboard. I watch the gathering wave carefully. It is what surfers call a 'peak' – a sudden pushing together of energy caused by a contoured sand bottom. The peak grows to an 'overhead' wave, taller than a person standing – more than 2 m (7 ft) high from trough to peak. Having watched the previous set of peaks from the beach, I know which wave – right or left – produces the best ride.

I swivel around on my board, still sitting (this is done by rotating one leg only in the water, like a propeller). Now the peak is conical, and approaching so fast that 'thought' is now an 'afterthought'. I'm running on instinct, adrenalin rushing through me, fully in the present, mindful, adaptive. The wave is still unbroken, or 'green', and is beginning to taper. I am paddling rapidly, one arm after another digging deep into the sea to gain maximum speed, all the while glancing behind me to make sure I am taking off in just the right spot for how I have read, and now hope to surf, the wave.

Within seconds I have made complex decisions about how much to angle the board away from the peak in the best direction for travel. The wave is now on my tail, and I jump smoothly to my feet in one unbroken movement, using my hands briefly to push me up and then rising on the thigh and calf muscles while my back straightens and my feet adjust with (for me, as I am what is called a 'natural foot') the left foot forward and the right foot back,

placed on the board in such a way that I shoot down the face of the wave, staying in the green, unbroken water, and smoothly arc the board at the base of the wave to face down the line – a 'bottom turn'. The board propels back up the face so that I seem to be heading almost skyward, dangerously close to flying. By a subtle adjustment of my weight I direct the left-hand side of the board down enough to bring me out of the turn and to track across the face. This is called 'trimming', or finding a 'line' on the wave – riding in the most critical or fastest-breaking part, yet staying on the green, unbroken water.

The Mindfulness Peak

Now comes a critical decision for an experienced longboard surfer. To push the limits I can get both of my feet close to the front of the board, preferably with five toes of one foot, or all ten toes for greatest effect and satisfaction, curled over the tip. This must be done without haste and with great elegance.

Along with the tuberide, this is the mindfulness peak for surfers, the moment of greatest 'reflection in the body' as perfect balance is achieved in a flash of apparent stillness while all around is actually moving at speed and promises to tip you off balance. This point of complete identification of mind with body, where the mind is absorbed by and continuous with the balance of the body, is surely what Buddhists describe as *bodhi* or 'awakening'. It is a mini-illumination, at-one-ness with nature. But it is a discipline achieved through practising mindfulness, and not by accident. And it is taught by the environment itself, shaping the senses from outside-in, as an ecological perception. *Bodhi* is necessarily a temporary state for all but the dedicated.

Surfing as a Calling

In Buddhism, the Threefold Way is described as yoking ethics, concentration and insight into daily activity. I have described the ethical way of ecological awareness rather than egological fascination, and above I describe some moments of concentration that can be achieved through practice. The shortfall for many is how does this translate into insight that is apparent in daily activity? The Threefold Way is sometimes seen as Buddha, Dharma and Sangha. The Buddha is the embodiment of ethics as natural law — of a morality that attunes with ecology. The Dharma is the dedicated path of those with a vocation, a calling. Here, I am suggesting that surfing can offer

Surfing can offer a calling as much as a more obvious spiritual teaching

that calling as much as a more obvious spiritual teaching. Sangha is to share that vocation in community and this is equivalent to 'insight'. It is the political, ethical and aesthetic calling to collaborate for the better life, for equality and justice, quality of life for all.

THE BODYMIND

◆

While the best longboard surfers have natural athletic ability, poise and cool, style does not come without the effort of many hours of practice. And here we come to the core of the book — what mindfulness can bring to surfing.

L ET US PUSH MINDFULNESS up a gear to 'the bodymind' or 'bodymindfulness', hinted at earlier. Elegant and apparently effortless longboard surfing would not happen just with mindfulness. It needs a mind in a body that is practised and reflexive. Donald Schön (1930–97) describes how experts in the professions (engineering and medicine in particular) gain expertise. It is not what you know that matters, but how the knowing is embodied in the 'doing' (thus 'being'). Further, it is the creative or innovative adaptation of knowing and being under conditions of uncertainty, ambiguity and uniqueness. This is where intuition comes in. Intuition is not a mystical state of inspiration but a hard-won state of expertise gained through practice.

In surfing, there are many things that you can predict beforehand. The size and movements of swells can be forecast days ahead from pressure and wind patterns studied on weather charts. The movement and shape of waves can be inferred from bottom conditions such as the contour of beaches, the size of gullies in sand made from current patterns, the nature of a coral reef, local geology, or the formation of pebbles in a 'point break', where waves peel off in a predictable fashion, often close to a headland. However much you can predict, there is always an unknown quantity and quality to the ways that waves break to which you must adapt at the time. This requires smooth innovation and on-the-spot experimentation, a wisdom gained from practice.

Only a Surfer Knows the Feeling

And, of course, there is a relationship to the equipment – the surfboard. Robert Pirsig's *Zen and the Art of Motorcycle Maintenance* describes a father looking after both a loved motorbike and a loved son. The medium for contemplation is the Zen-like state – both people and machines need careful, loving attention and more, contemplation. Unlike a motorbike, a surfboard has no moving parts. It is clearly not as complicated. Unlike flesh and blood, losing a surfboard is relatively meaningless. Perhaps I should not pursue links between contemplation and a surfboard, sold as if one could stroke it. But 'stroke it' is precisely what a surfer wants to do when they handle a surfboard.

'Only a surfer knows the feeling' is a common expression for the joy of riding waves, but only a surfer knows the feeling of a new board. It becomes a positive fetish object. When transferred to wave surfaces, skittering along a green, glassy wall, the board engages in conversation and becomes friend

or enemy, depending upon its performance. The board is animated, personified. It outgrows both its utility and its presence as an art object as you push it to its limits, or rather, it pushes you to your limits as you wipeout.

Coping with Panic & the Wipeout

The ancient Greeks described Pan, the god of nature ('pan' literally means 'everything'), as a hairy, horny, smelly goat god who, just as you are at your most satisfied in the middle of the day when the sun is overhead, jumps on your back to create pan-ic. Of course, at this point you cast no shadow; it has disappeared into your body or it is fully absorbed. Just at the point when you thought you were most in control, in cruise control, panic attacks you. For many people, this simply throws them off course. For experts, this moment is absorbed in a flash, creatively distilled and the residue discarded, in what we call a moment of intuitive brilliance. Let us call this a bodymindfulness at work at the still centre of stormy activity. Let us expand the catchphrase 'Only a surfer knows the feeling' to suggest that the ordinary moment of panic can be turned into an extraordinary moment of reflection-as-action, instinct, or psychological reflection.

The ancient Greeks tell of the relationships between Pan the goat god (born wrapped in the pelt of a hare and abandoned by his mother), Echo a wood nymph and Narcissus a mortal. Echo (best thought of as psychological reflection)

Caught Between Fish & Bird

When I was a kid, my dad told me a Maori folk tale about a big-headed villager who boasted that he could bring home a whale that would feed the whole community for a winter. The young man tricked the whale into letting him ride it, just like a surfboard, lulling the whale into going straight into shore so that it beached itself and died. The whale was a totem animal for the neighbouring village and they were shocked when they heard how the whale had been tricked, as they would never eat their totem or treat it badly. Many surfers may be just like the big-headed villager – unaware of how their activities mistreat the environment and how we abuse our animal relatives. Mindful surfers would have the opposite mindset – respectful of sea life and acutely aware of the environment. They would live somewhere between fish and bird, sitting on their surfboards.

There is a powerful lesson to be learned from all sea life, so well adapted. Humans work against currents and winds, powering machines to journey in the straightest possible line. But this is hugely inefficient. Turtles and sharks use the currents to travel. Dolphins in pods leap so high because they work collaboratively to produce strong vortices and eddies in the water that supplement their muscle power, allowing them to burst higher and further than their body mass should allow.

Lighter than cork

I danced on waves

in the salt air.

FROM 'THE DRUNKEN BOAT'
ARTHUR RIMBAUD, FRENCH POET, 1854–91

falls in love with Narcissus, but is spurned as Narcissus becomes entirely fixated by his own reflection and not by the echoes of nature (perhaps the wind and crashing waves). This tale suggests that narcissism or self-interest is a curse of our age that turns us away from conversation with the natural world, where the echo might be called the teachings of nature (such as what will a breaking wave or a fast-moving current teach you?). Echo, however, refuses the affection of Pan, suggesting to us that reflection and instinct are hard to bring together in conversation and that this has to be achieved through practice and technique (how do you 'listen' to the wave?). In myth, Pan gets so frustrated with Echo that he tears her into many pieces and throws her to the wind, where we still hear her today.

Is this a story suggesting that blind panic or anxiety must be tempered with reflection? What do we learn from our inevitable mistakes as we take on the challenge of surfing? Practice is defined by perfecting a bodymind, a reflection in the body, and not just muscle or cognition.

OCEAN SWELL

First Ride

One of the most thrilling experiences in surfing is to witness someone standing upright on a wave for the very first time. My cousin Paul had suffered a stroke that affected both his speech and the left side of his body. His legs remained healthy and although he could no longer work, he began to run, participating in daily circuits near his home on the King's Road in London and eventually in marathons. He visited me in Cornwall, and although his speech was slow, with time he could express himself. Over breakfast he made me laugh when he described the grinding sound of the sea at night as being similar to the constant hum of London traffic.

I took Paul surfing, expecting that without the strength in his left arm he would have to ride (lying) prone to the shore on each wave. At the best of times, just standing on the board for a beginner can be like trying to ride a cricket bat down a rapid. Add the cold, oily waters of the North Atlantic turbine into the mix and the baptism of surfing can be tough. I got Paul to lie on the board, waited for a wave and pushed him into the breaking foam. He rode it all the way to the beach lying down and when I caught up with him, he was wearing a huge smile.

Six rides later, with a little help from me – alongside and supporting him – Paul stood up. The board made a raunchy, buzzing sound and this, I knew, would be an unforgettable experience for Paul. As the wave faded out, he fell safely into

the shallow water. That ride challenged every skill of balance and timing. The smile stayed on Paul's face for the rest of the day – the immediate impact of immersion in nature. It releases the playful child inside, stimulates our senses and awakens our wonder. This, in turn, shifts our attention and makes room for creativity and calm to come to the fore.

Badge of Honour

But stepping in also means wiping out – an immediate cause of panic. The first physical experience in surfing for many will be the wipeout, often at the breaking point of the wave, where you try to rise to your feet, only to be utterly swallowed in the guts of the swirling water. But wipeouts can also be treated as a badge of honour. They are repeated endlessly in surfers' lore, exaggerated and embellished. Yes, they can literally wipe out a surfer's career, or dent it badly. But most wipeouts are harmless and part of the fun of surfing. The first thing every surfer must learn is to deal with the panic of the wipeout, turning this into a positive. Every time you wipeout, immediately cradle your head by wrapping both arms around, thus protecting it from the board, which might decide to dart straight for you. Thankfully, surf lessons are usually performed on beach breaks where you can safely press your feet into the sand, wade out to catch a wave in waist-deep water, and enjoy all the experiences of immersion in nature and mindfulness that surfing demands.

COASTLINES AS CHARACTERS

◆

Surfing educates acute sensitivity to coastline, developing sense-based observational skills. Do you see how the world shapes perception and not the other way around? 'Eco' precedes 'ego'. Surfing along (and within) a coastline leads us and informs us.

WHILE THE PSYCHOLOGIST James Gibson describes the perspective of 'ecological perception', the French-Caribbean poet Saint-John Perse writes in *Anabasis* about the great forces of nature – thunder, lightning, wind, lashing rain and, above all, the tides and the ocean swells (but also the big, empty silences of calm skies and tranquil seas) – shaping character and perception as an affordance. This outside-in view of 'ecological perception' is resurrected in the philosophical position of Externalism, again suggesting that the environment shapes the way we see it through 'affordance' of features, rather than us acting on the environment. These theories challenge subject as agent, suggesting that persons are 'subject to' environment and enjoy an embedding in the world as extended cognition and embodiment. This position reframes the coastline, where the environment educates us to see its 'interiority'. This perceptual art allows us to appreciate the interior lives as well as the exterior expressions of coastlines, and to be taught by coastlines as characters. Perhaps a better term for the character of coastline is 'coastscape'.

MINDFULNESS EXERCISE

BEING AT THE BEACH

No matter how stressed I feel, or how crammed I am with concerns and worries, just stepping into the ever-changing flux of the sea clears my mind. All I can do is respond and react. I cannot control that flux, but I can get to understand it and adapt to its flows and moods. Very rarely will a thought enter my mind not connected to the moving environment that surrounds me, a water duvet doubling over as I slip into surfsleep – perhaps to dream of a perfect wave! And when a thought does enter my mind, I will sense it, and easily be able to let it move away (if it is not connected to the here and now). This is bodymindfulness in action.

I feel immediately relaxed when I arrive at my local beach. But of course often beaches are busy, packed with visitors, perhaps your usual sitting spot now taken. Let all those frustrations wash over you. Mindfulness is about observation without criticism. If busy beaches really frustrate you, visit them early or late in the day, or enjoy them in the off-season as a perfect antidote to a winter depression.

Here are simple ways to be mindful at the beach before you paddle out:
* Go barefoot and stand upright, or sit comfortably, with a strong, straight spine. For people with a disability who cannot do this, adopt the most comfortable posture and know that surfing is going to be therapeutic. Feel every grain of sand between your toes.
* The beach may be noisy, either from people chatting, kids playing, or surf or wind blowing. Absorb this sound as it is part of the brilliant energy of place. Let it inspire calm as your breath provides a regulatory pulse. Move out to the common commotion rather than inwards, cutting off from it. Oddly enough, you will find a still centre at the heart of the commotion or buzz.
* This is the perfect time to read the sea, or the 'line up' as surfers call it. Spot the rip currents (where the incoming energy of waves drains back to

deep water) that can help you paddle out. Notice where the waves are breaking and where other surfers are sitting. But it should not take a crowd to make a crowd. If you spot a location that is empty, but looks safe and is a recognized surfing area, paddle out there. Be aware of the environment and the presence of other surfers.

• Never beat yourself up about your progress in surfing. Mindful surfing is not about success or failure. It is about replacing frantic 'doing' with mindful 'being'. Let the sea revive exhaustion, enjoy the wipeout, turn the frustration of the crowded surf into happiness and just being in the sea. Let your time in the surf evoke creativity and mental clarity. It is amazing how in the sea you forget everything. Then you remember on land. The beach is a zone of cleansing for me. Ask surfers fresh from the water what they were thinking about in the waves and you immediately witness that they have been in a state of mindfulness as they look at you in puzzlement.

Summary

Let the beach be a zone of adjustment to turn from doing to being, whatever your level of proficiency or capability. Feel the sand between your toes. Follow your natural breathing cycle. Emerge in the present, close noticing the surf and fellow surfers. Then paddle out to surf safely, and stay in tune. Never immerse in yourself – that is the ego at work; always immerse in the environment, letting the eco take off and take over.

Visualize, for a moment, an ocean experience. Maybe not surfing, but perhaps swimming at a beach during the high tide. The deep-water surge begins to pull you back and forth, so that you fight violently to stabilize yourself, afraid of being dragged under. Then something tells you to put off struggling. You look to shore and realize the proximity to the beach, the cove, the cliffs and safety. You then feel stable in the surge, as part of the surge. You drown the will to fight against the movement. And then, the links of light reflecting blue on the surface of the sea begin to delight you. You swim in, revived. Things started awkwardly, but the environment captured your attention. You let go, mindful. A new noticing emerged; the coastscape became the character, on display. This is body-mindfulness. And bodymindfulness, as explored in this book, is a morality attuned ecologically and shared in a community: Buddha, Dharma, Sangha.

Facing the Other

While surf travel engages intimately with coastscape, such a possessive taxis is dangerous, replaying the imperial gaze of the conqueror who, historically, has appropriated coastscapes and shaped them to his (the conqueror is gendered male) desires. In the histories of a variety of colonialisms, these movements, this circular path of coastal landing to interior and movement back to coast, is where the Other – the stranger and the strange – is demonized. But of course it is you – the visiting surfer and traveller – who is the stranger and not the stronger. This cultural movement, this desire to conquer and teach rather than to learn, leads to exploitation of resources including the human, as seen in the history of the slave trade through waves of colonialism and neocolonialism.

Polish travel writer Ryszard Kapuściński (1932–2007) reversed the colonial gaze, so that his identity was formed in response to an Other. Reporting on the independence movement of Africa in the mid to late twentieth century, Kapuściński distilled a philosophy, summed up in *The Other*, familiar from the work of Emmanuel Levinas (1906–95), who pondered the consequences of the Holocaust. Kapuściński's travels taught him tolerance and respect for the Other, just as Levinas sought a way to forgiveness after the Holocaust.

> *The greatest ethical challenge is to 'face' the Other*

Levinas promoted a radical philosophy of identity – that we do not have an essential self to which we can return as a reference point. Rather, self is only ever known in the face of the Other, as an appreciation of difference. The greatest ethical challenge is to 'face' the Other, so that relationships can be formed in a world of such wide cultural differences. Kapuściński models what the travel writer Tony Hiss calls 'deep travel', describing the feeling that wherever we are, everything can come alive, or be seen anew. A second sense is restored, an animal sense or animalizing imagination.

The Environmental 'Other'

And how about challenging the notion that the 'Other' has to be a human Other, suggesting instead that the environment itself can be the mirror of the Other in which a self is discovered? One of the most poetic and sensitive writers exploring this line of thinking and being is the American philosopher and anthropologist Alphonso Lingis. He chose to visit areas where there was potential danger or hazard, physically or emotionally, to investigate ideas that became the stark and bold titles for his books: *Excesses, Foreign Bodies, Abuses, Dangerous Emotions, Violence and Splendor*. Exploring big ideas – love, trust, death, lust – through contextually local narratives, these themes are considered in extreme situations such as dishevelled urbanscapes, backwaters, jails.

Lingis remembers extreme situations in writing through the tone of the body, where the reader cannot help but make connections between thought and physicality. Surfing is a constant interplay between feeling and mindfulness. Lingis brings muscle to the academic's mind and finesse to the explorer's muscle, always crossing boundaries.

Phenomenology is a branch of modern philosophy that attempts to describe phenomena – the world of appearances – 'as they are', unmediated by intellectual filters. Phenomenologists ask themselves – how can we best allow the world of objects to shine forth? Preconceptions and the intellectual apparatus are 'bracketed out' in an attempt to let the world

present itself – not as it 'is' (a truth assumption that phenomenology does not make), but how it 'appears' to the senses.

Lingis would enjoy surfing because it is a sensuous experience. This demands risk. I am aware that 'living dangerously'
may be a male-gendered notion, following writers such as
Kapuściński and Ernest Hemingway (1899–1961) who might
believe that the best education for journalism is to visit a war
zone. Lingis is not a stereotypical macho warrior adventurer,
but rather follows Nietzsche's view that to 'live dangerously'
is also to think dangerously. Nietzsche (1844–1900) also
pointed out how the world in which we live directs us to act,
in an idea of ecological perception preceding James Gibson.

The 'Other' on Your Doorstep

Kapuściński and Lingis teach us that the 'Other' can be many
things – place, people, point of view. The point is to celebrate
difference. But the Other is not necessarily the foreign.
The Other can be the unusual, the original, even the familiar.
You can find the Other on your doorstep, in a new mindset, or in
trying surfing for the first time. Surfing demystifies the exotic,
the heroic, and challenges the imperial through a celebration
of sense-based experience and cultural exchange. Suspension of
the imperialistic 'I' will hopefully allow the character of places
to shine. The land, sky and sea have personality and so do coastlines themselves. Surfing is mindfulness in action as a close
noticing and a lifting of culture-bound preconceptions.

CHAPTER THREE

DROPPING IN

I know a keen surfer when I see one.
I can read it in the eyes, a clear deep sense of
mindfulness. Before and after dropping into the wave,
surfers might reflect and philosophize; and they are
first and foremost expert phenomenologists. They notice
things, deeply and closely. They crave experience
without mediation of theory; yet they develop intuitive
knowledge about the geography of their favourite
activity, such as how waves are formed and how beaches
change shape. Despite being stereotyped as brain-
numbed hedonists, surfers can be thinkers.

BLUE MINDS

◆

Surfers have, historically, cultivated body over mind. Surfing is first and foremost sensual. But surfers have to be thinkers too, obsessively checking weather patterns, a long way from the motto on an old surfing T-shirt of mine: 'No Brains, No Headaches.'

OF COURSE, THERE ARE TELLTALE SIGNS of a surfer: bloodshot eyes (from salt and sun), tight back muscles (from paddling), wind-chapped lips. The language can be an immediate giveaway. Listening to surfers talk about surfing is an extraordinary guide to close noticing. First, there is the surfer's interest in the texture of the waves. Surfers, of course, *surf* the *face* of the wave, offering a model of connectivity to the sea's *surface*. The environment educates the body sensually. Surfing is about close observation of the surprisingly delicate and sensuous events embedded in otherwise challenging environments. The experiences recounted have involved meditating, smelling, listening, feeling, being sensitive to nature's body as a whole. That is a basic spiritual path. It is not a path meant to exclude or divide, it is about sharing, acceptance and cultural exchange. Surfers often talk as if they have found a secret in life, describing sea states and ocean experiences, tides and memorable rides for hours. The tone is often as if the best is yet to come, no matter what the age, excited by the future because there is a new swell forecast.

Narrative of the Dream Glide

There is serious academic study of surfing, a 'surfology', embodied in the pioneering Surf Science and Technology BSc degree developed at the University of Plymouth (and still running at Cornwall College), including coastal geomorphology and physical science, history of the sport, study of the lifestyle, commodification of surfing, sociology, equipment engineering, industry issues and the leisure and tourism business. The detailed oceanographic understanding of coastal processes has translated into a collection of surfing guidebooks with accurate travel information, seasonal surfing insight, generic surf histories and local folklore. A scientific understanding (meteorology and forecasting surfing conditions) is driven by a quest to find the perfect wave, showcased in the first wide-appeal surfing film – *The Endless Summer* (1966).

There is also a growing social and cultural literature that has issues of space, place and identity construction as its main interests. There is an artistic aspect of surfing, with reference to style, idiosyncratic characters shaping a lifestyle, poetic questions about the 'feel' of a board or a wave, not just its technical dimensions. Surfing has an expressive side and this is just as open to study and debate. *Surfing and Social Theory: Experience, Embodiment and Narrative of the Dream Glide* by Nick Ford and David Brown is the first sustained commentary on the contemporary social and cultural meaning of surfing. Ford and Brown explore themes of mind and body, emotions and

identity, aesthetics, style, and sensory experience. They contextualize surfing by tracking evolving historical perceptions of the sea and the beach, to provide an analysis of issues such as embodiment in, and gendering of, surfing.

The Poetics of Water

These works unconsciously echo the 'poetics of water' described by the French phenomenologist and scientist Gaston Bachelard (1884–1962). Bachelard's essay on the imagination of matter makes water matter in a poetic way, as a medium for dreaming or reverie. University of Cambridge French lecturer Andy Martin has written two books about surfing, exploring the metamorphosis that surfing, proximity to the ocean, or stardom in the sport can induce and the trace that this leaves. Martin slides easily from popular surf culture to high culture and philosophical discourse, providing a commentary on sport and psyche.

Martin has experienced heavy whitewater hold-downs in Hawaiian waves, while his academic credibility is high and his journalistic crankiness and humour are refreshing. Bearing

---

The sea possesses a power over one's moods

that has the effect of a will. The sea can hypnotize.

FROM 'THE LADY FROM THE SEA'
HENRIK IBSEN, NORWEGIAN PLAYWRIGHT, 1828–1906

---

an uncanny resemblance to the late French philosopher and founder of deconstruction Jacques Derrida (1930–2004), Martin has forged an original aesthetic in surf literature. He manages to find fault lines and points of tension in surf culture. In a short surf film for *The Independent* online (*Once Upon a Time in New York*), Martin, the narrator, says:

> Steven Kotler has argued (in his book West of Jesus: Science, Surfing, and the Origins of Belief) *that there is a neurochemistry of surfing that tends to produce a heightened receptivity to feelings of transcendence. Perhaps there is no activity that is not potentially philosophical, but it has always seemed to me that the collision of (as Sartre would say) the in-itself (the wave) and the for-itself (the surfer), with all its possible outcomes of pleasure and pain (the wipeout and the hold-down), and especially the tuberide, with its narrative of being buried and then (ideally) reborn, naturally gives rise to a contemplative state.*

We might enlarge the connections to suggest that the coastscape is the fabric of transcendence, holding the surfer in its field. Perhaps surfing is neither sport nor recreation, but what the late poet, novelist and lay psychoanalyst Peter Redgrove (1932–2003) called a 'hole-in-the-day' (a pun on 'holiday'), an everyday opportunity for transcendence. Surfing is less the contemplation of such connections than the voicing of these connections, an uttered celebration of the hole-in-the-day, or a grappling with opportunity.

Flow State

In *Blue Mind*, marine biologist and surfer Wallace J. Nichols describes his collaborative work with neuroscientists, psychologists, economists and athletes, examining the impact of being in or near water. They demonstrate that proximity to water can improve focus, creativity, health and professional success and gives rise to what Nichols calls a 'blue mind', a neurological state causing a sense of calm centredness. The book was launched at the annual Blue Mind conference, which in 2014 was held in Mawgan Porth, Cornwall. In the opening lecture, Nichols explained the difference between directed attention (when we deliberately focus) and involuntary attention (when an external stimulus captures our attention). He argued that being around water heightens involuntary attention, generating a blue mind. Consequently, neurochemicals such as dopamine (pleasure), serotonin (peace) and endorphins (euphoria) are released.

Nichols continued, 'Juxtaposed to blue mind is red mind, when your neurons release norepinephrine, cortisol and glucocorticoid in response to stress, anxiety and fear. Surfing benefits from both a blue and red mind, but experienced surfers are able to turn red mind (such as the fear of the wipeout) to blue mind. The…more we surf, the more efficient we become at recognizing the flux of water and movement of waves, and positioning and reacting accordingly. Ultimately the surfer can unconsciously respond in the blink of an eye to changing conditions. This is flow state, when we lose track of time, nothing else seems to matter, and we truly seem alive and at our best.'

Surfing stimulates the muscles, releases energy, removes stress and increases the flow of oxygen to the brain so that you return in a different state of 'being', and above all the 'doing' changes your 'being'. Surfing a coastscape over time also produces a deep spatial knowledge that becomes a kind of shared container for learning about the environment. While much of the rhetoric of surfing appears macho or martial (such as 'killing' a wave), surfers tend to think spatially (an archetypal feminine attribute) rather than temporally (an archetypal masculine attribute) and this spatial thinking is embodied and affords subjectivities. Surfers also tend to think both socially or collaboratively, in identification as a group with a particular location or surfing break. Here, the material environment affords a kind of sensuality that constructs an identity as a keen observer of wave shapes, winds and currents. 'Surfing spaces' generates a feminine connectedness with coastscape and performative space that is subjectifying, rather than a masculine gaze that distances and is objectifying. Importantly, surfing acts as an aesthetic impulse. In summary, as well as thinking with surfing in mind, surfers can also be thinkers.

Surfing stimulates the muscles, releases energy, removes stress ...

Tideline

Standing on the cliff edge at Gwenver, scanning from Land's End to the south and all the way to Cape Cornwall to the north, it is a stunning day for the gods to hang out their laundry across cobalt blue skies. I can smell and practically taste the coconut and pineapple (with a hint of vanilla) haze drifting from acres of gorse across the fields. Hobbies hover, smaller than kestrels and swift-like in appearance, eyeing small prey. Swallows are swooping around the wet rocks at one end of the tideline. There are ribbons of seaweed. It is warming up, but there is still a chill in the air as it is only just breaking free from spring. In the background is a grinding sound. There is a deep swell running. The sea is racing to deposit its entire weight on the beach below in pulses. The sets are wrapping in cadence. Importantly there is a big spring tide, the result of an increase in the gravitational pull on the ocean when the sun and moon align. The extra energy is more than tangible. Quite simply, the combined effect of the moon and sun varies throughout the month. When the moon and sun are working with each other (at full moon and new moon), this produces the largest tidal ranges (spring tides). At so-called 'first quarter' and 'last quarter' the moon and sun work against each other, resulting in smaller tidal ranges (neap tides).

Surfing for me celebrates not only a sense of place, but also the energy and movement around this place, a rhythmic engagement with coastscape and tides and the fluidity and surprise of swells coming and going. The steep ascent down the cliff path is a regular journey, today bathed in reflected light from the sea. Some days are full of luminous white. Just the burs of burdock can be made out, as if to shout 'I am alive'. Other days I spot the beds of stinging nettles, the spectacular sand dunes, the orchestra of skylarks, the pounding shorebreak, the incessant tidal layers. This singing out of place is part of surfing as mindfulness.

Surfing then becomes not just about riding the wave, but immersion in nature: the aching silence of a calm sea is punctuated by a cluster of blue lines. Then, after the set of waves passes, a big space opens up, and there is, again, a familiar calm. The point is to spend a little more time looking and listening before doing. Maybe this is not just about being but about what the philosopher Martin Heidegger (1889–1976) called 'becoming' – a being in time, an unfolding sense of what he further called 'dwelling'. When we dwell, we inhabit. I try to notice how some things only come with certain tides and cluster after certain winds, watching where the cormorants dive for fish: it always seems to be the spot where the wave energy is highest.

MINDFULNESS AND SURFING

GEOGRAPHICAL IMAGINATION

We all have to travel to surf – a short walk, a long drive or perhaps a trip abroad. But surf travel must begin with a geographical imagination – a kind of psychogeography that gets inside the mind of a place.

BRITISH GEOGRAPHER AND SURFER Nick Ford first coined the term 'coastscape' to collectively describe coastal landscape, seascape and culture. Surf travel educates acute sensitivity to coastscape and, importantly, to movement. The rhythmic engagement with coastlines, again elegantly explored by the poet Saint-John Perse as the cycle of *anabasis* (moving from coast to interior) and *katabasis* (interior to coast), is central to surf travel.

Geography, literally 'writing out the earth', explores relationships between space, place and identity and this triangulation is common in travel. The notion of the geographical imagination was developed by the Marxist geographer Doreen Massey to give meaning to location. This also characterizes 'psychogeography' – getting inside the 'mind' of a place as much as the people who inhabit places. Psychogeography has recently been popularized by novelists such as Iain Sinclair and Will Self. The Mexican-born philosopher Manuel de Landa has developed a further stream of psychogeography in tracing a life history of the earth through physical processes, informed

CELEBRATING THE SALT STAIN

The French poet laureate Saint-John Perse described a tidemark – on a beach as the high tide strand line, or as a stain on a harbour wall – as a 'salt stain' that cannot be erased. Those who surf regularly have a permanent print or tidemark on the psyche – not just the mark of time, but of time well spent. The 'tideline' of surfing is also physical as a salt-stain residue left on the skin after every dip in the ocean. Salt is the very taste of surfing, and every coastline has a particular flavour.

As a kind of 'thank you' ritual for the freely given gift of the surf, walk out of the water with a mindset – imagine that you are breaking free from the welcome grip of the ocean that is provided by its oily and very thin skin, and as you leave so the skin heals and forms over behind you. Your intuitive 'breaking out' of the skin of the sea as a farewell gesture may be a real sensation of one skin rubbing against another in a common understanding and common project of care.

Further, why not (just this time) forget the freshwater shower and enjoy that salt stain on the skin. Of course, this is interrupted in cold water through wearing a wetsuit. Do not let that bother you – imagine the wetsuit as a sealskin, making entry and exit from the water as a breaking and healing of the ocean's skin even smoother.

Summary
As you leave the water, pause for a moment and remember that you are breaking free of the skin of the sea, to which you have just been joined. Allow the sea's skin to settle back into shape and enjoy the sensation of salt stain on your own skin. If you are wearing a wetsuit, become a seal in the process. The uppermost 1 millimetre of the ocean, effectively its skin, is a gelatinous, sticky film full of microbial life, unique to this layer, that may be important to the wellbeing of the planet.

by complexity theory. This 'cultural geomorphology' suggests that the physical environment, as a deep and slow-moving historical process, shapes us. These ideas resonate with the philosophical perspective of Externalism and the psychology of 'ecological perception'.

The Map in the Mind

In psychogeography, the map in the mind is as important as the cartographer's document, but also the physical surroundings are animated or given voice. The history of Western philosophy is largely one of movement from perception of an animated environment to description of an inner self. For example, the British poet and author Ruth Padel shows how the ancient Greek mind saw the world as animated and acting upon humans, so that, for example, an external force creates feeling in the liver (*thymos* or 'blood soul') or the lungs (*phrenes* or 'breath soul'). So, the air literally acts on the lungs and the result is inspiration or animation, an uplifting feeling of lightness. In contrast, what is felt from outside in the liver is a pooling of blood, a heaviness or earthing, a movement of the soul rather than the spirit.

These ancient ideas challenge the modern notion of subject as agent, suggesting that persons are, rather, 'subject to' environment and enjoy an embedding in the world as extended cognition and embodiment. This new form of the geographical imagination, as a form of Externalism, reframes the identity of the author, whose self is neither given nor expressed, but whose multiple selves are constituted according to environment, including acute sensitivity to the 'Other' in celebration of difference.

The Cycle of Anabasis-Katabasis

Saint-John Perse's 1924 poem *Anabasis* describes the movement of imperialists keen to uproot and claim new territory, who may just be captured by the spirit of the nomad and refuse new territorializing. Perse's poem is loosely based on the ancient Greek writer and warrior Xenophon's *Anabasis*, the Greek word for an expedition from a coastline to the interior of a country. Travelling surfers, however, move in the opposite direction, from the interior to the coast. The Greek term for this was *katabasis*. And the mindful method of surf travel is to sensitively explore the cycle of *anabasis-katabasis*. This involves being in the present and appreciating the varieties of cultures and ways of life that present themselves as affordances shaping perception, character and imagination; and resisting the imperialist urge 'to conquer' or territorialize. This round of movement from interior to coast and coast to interior is like the rise and fall of the lung in a steady breathing cycle, or like the beating of the heart.

*Resisting the imperialist
urge to territorialize*

CHAPTER FOUR

SURFING WITH
THE ANCIENTS

*In Polynesia, where surfing began, the
Hawaiian* he'e nalu *was used to describe 'wave
sliding' — the relationship between wave, board and
rider. A wave is liquid, fast-moving and heavy — it can
easily break a surfboard in two as it lumps up then tips
over, where green water turns to white foam. Surfers too
momentarily adopt a liquid form as they ride to shore.
This liquidity of body — and elasticity of mind — is
key to mindfulness. And the type of board you ride
is vital to such a mindful experience. Riding
any surfboard immediately grounds
you in a rich history.*

HAWAII:
A BRIEF HISTORY OF SURFING

◆

Growing up in Newquay in the 1950s, my dad and his friends rode 'bellyboards' before surfboards proper appeared on the scene, failing to realize the connection to tropical Polynesia — not surprising in the cool-water Atlantic.

BELLYBOARD SURFING, riding prone on short, wooden, curved-nose boards, is three to four thousand years old. It appeared independently along the coastlines of West Africa and all around the Pacific from New Guinea to Easter Island. In Peru, a unique style of reed canoe was developed that was probably surfed standing up. Wave-riding became embedded in the Polynesian cultures of New Zealand, Tahiti and Marquesas. When these ocean-roaming Polynesians settled in *Owhyhee* (the 'Homeland' of 'Hawaii') in 400CE, stand-up surfing really started. The environment was ideal for deep-water swells to break on shallow water reefs, creating steep, powerful waves. A plethora of board designs allowed expert riders to manoeuvre on the slope of the wave face.

The Olo

Big, bruising *Olo* boards (reserved for Hawaiian royalty) were between 5.5 and 6 metres (18 and 20 feet) in length, so would have taken several people to carry down the beach to launch.

I often imagine this challenge just carrying some of my heavier surfboards down to my local beach at Gwenver. I paddle out, reliving the sport of kings and queens of Hawaii in cold but perfectly clear water. The Cornish rinse is bracing and where I live in the far reaches of the county had its traditions of royalty like Hawaii, but much earlier. The Land's End peninsula is dotted with Neolithic burial mounds, now exposed as granite quoits, each protecting a royal tomb. Surfing was the sport of Polynesian kings and queens because only royalty were allowed to ride these big *Olo* boards. Surfing was hierarchical, not even a meritocracy (where the best riders could claim the best boards) and certainly not a democracy as it is today, where any level of surfer can own any kind of board.

The Alaia

Most *maka'ainana* (common) Hawaiians rode prone on short *Paipo* boards, or standing on 2.5-metre-long (8 feet) *Alaias*. They were made from the koa (acacia) or ulu (breadfruit) tree, less buoyant than the prized wiliwili wood (used for the *Olo*). Expert boardmakers searched the forests for sound trees, felled them and shaped them on the spot with stone and bone tools. Boards were customized for the rider, carefully worked with adzes and coral sanding blocks. They were polished with stones and stained with vegetable dyes such as the ti plant, banana buds or burnt pandanus leaves. Finally they were glossed with kukui nut oil and then blessed and ridden.

After the surf, the board was dried in the sun and rubbed with coconut oil to preserve the wood, wrapped in tapa cloth and suspended inside the house to prevent sun and insect damage. The board became a prized family member.

Work Not Play

One of the first European accounts of surfing in coral-rich waters appears in the official journals of the Captain James Cook expeditions. In *A Voyage to the Pacific Ocean: Volume III*, Lieutenant James King devoted two pages to Hawaiian surfers. King would not have known at the time, but surfing was nearly killed off in Hawaii following British colonial contact. Imported diseases such as chicken pox, cholera and syphilis practically crippled the home of wave-riding. The Hawaiian population dropped drastically – from 300,000 in the mid-eighteenth century to 70,000 by the mid-nineteenth century. To add insult to injury, in the face of the Calvinist philosophy of 'work not play' brought by Christian missionaries, surfing was seen as frivolous and apparently 'against the laws of God', especially as it was conducted semi- or wholly naked.

But surfing survived the stifling puritan embrace. A small number of non-conformist Hawaiians – such as Chief Abner Paki – kept surfing alive in the 1800s by riding waves in secret. Almost 2 m (over 6 ft) tall, Chief Abner Paki was a 140 kilo (22 stone) giant of a man. His 5.5 m (18 ft) *Olo* board can still be seen at the Bishop Museum in Honolulu.

Waikiki Renaissance

Ultimately, surfing was wholeheartedly revived in Hawaii as tourism and beach culture became popularized for the affluent in the early 1900s. The ancient sport of Hawaii – now annexed territory of the USA – became a symbol for American tourists to consume, as a mark of a healthy lifestyle. The economy switched from sugar (which had brought 75,000 Japanese to the islands to work in the cane fields between 1898 and 1907) to tourism. An electric trolley took tourists down from Honolulu, about 5 km (3 miles) from Waikiki – a frangipani-lined beach where the trade winds blow perfectly offshore, combing waves clean.

Waikiki is Hawaiian for 'spouting water' and became the renaissance surf break, home to international surfing emissaries Duke Kahanamoku (1890–1968) and George Freeth (1883–1919). Two hotels – the Moana (opened in 1901) and the Seaside (1906) – offered surf lessons from the emerging group of local Waikiki beach boys (Duke had five surfing brothers) who lived by an old Hawaiian proverb: '*Hõ a'e ka 'ike he'e nalu i ka hokua o ka 'ale'* – 'Show (your) knowledge of surfing on the back of the wave.' The 'back' of the wave here is the curl, at the back of the surfer.

The surfing revival also included a revival of other sacred Hawaiian arts, including hula, a living theatre that accompanied an oral tradition of poetry and was often danced for Pele the fire goddess. There were 300 distinct hulas in the

Hawaiian repertoire before colonial contact. Tourism presented a market for beach lifeguarding, surf lessons and professional hula troupes, entertaining locals and visitors at *luaus* (outdoor parties). Hawaiian music was also re-energized, using intricate drumming templates, split bamboo sticks, gourd rattles, castanet pebbles and hardwood sticks. Famously, imported guitars and ukuleles had their strings 'slackened' to suit traditional Hawaiian songs, giving a laid-back feel. Waikiki beach boys played a finger-picking style with a steady rhythm to accompany singing and hula dancing and surfing. Imagine the beauty and grace of the enigmatic Duke Kahanamoku as he surfed, a local swimming champion with a perfectly honed body, chiselled features and swept-back hair. The slack key guitar and its tones echoed the laconic style of traditional Hawaiian surfing, where grace was held above aggression as the main virtue of classy surfers. Even the wipeout must be graceful. The surfer pops up, not in an angry lather but thankful that the gods have spared him or her.

Hui Nalu

The island's best local surfers, swimmers, paddlers and canoe-racers, including George Freeth and Duke Kahanamoku, founded the Hui Nalu (Club of Waves) in 1908. They became one with sea life: 'I see the sharks all the time,' said Duke, who swam well out to sea in daily practice. 'I don't bother them and they don't bother me.'

Duke earned a place in the American swimming team for the 1912 Olympics in Stockholm. He won gold in the 100 metres freestyle, and was catapulted to fame. Subsequently, he won gold in the same race in 1920 in Antwerp (there were no Games in 1916) and silver in 1924 in Paris (the 'Chariots of Fire' Olympics), where his brother Samuel won bronze. Invited to give swimming exhibitions around the world, Duke travelled with a surfboard, a 3-metre-long (10 feet) *Alaia*. Duke was recognized internationally as the emissary of surfing, solidifying a reputation of expert Hawaiian watermen and women. He even reintroduced surfing (once the sport of the Maori) to New Zealand in 1915.

Hawaii became a new magnet for travel writers. In his glory days as a bestselling adventure novelist – *The Call of the Wild*, *The Sea Wolf* and *White Fang* – Jack London was taught to surf by George Freeth in 1907. In the same year, Freeth was hired by the Pacific Electric railroad to introduce surfing to Los Angeles through a cunning marketing scheme. The company hoped to lure the public into making regular trips to the Pacific in its railway carriages. At Redondo Beach, and other spots along the Southern Californian coast, Freeth gave demonstrations and lessons to spark interest among young Californians. Beach culture would boom here.

*Even the wipeout
must be graceful*

Duke Inspires Australia

In 1915, Duke was invited to Australia to compete against their champions in pool meets. The swells poured in daily along the eastern coastline. In Sydney, Duke visited a timber firm, carved a length of sugar pine and surfed at Freshwater Beach. He picked out sixteen-year-old Isabel Letham from a large crowd and quickly got her up and riding, tandem and then solo: Australia's first stand-up wonder. Claude West was also taught that day. After Duke left, West became Australia's long-term surf champion. With thousands of miles of coastline and an already established beach lifesaving culture, surfing was a natural step for a sports-loving and competitive nation.

Letham left Australia to pursue a career in Hollywood, eventually taking up American citizenship. Later in life, she would remark how opportunities for women in the period between the world wars in Australia were severely limited, where California, in contrast, was liberated. Duke also travelled and surfed through Southern California and worked in Hollywood, playing Indian chiefs and island locals. Surfing cultivated that frontier spirit – innovation and a desire for self-expression and freedom from rules.

Lifeguard Tom Blake would become the next emissary of surfing. Blake was a design visionary. He created the first hollow wooden boards and added a fin in 1935 for directional stability. This was a hugely significant breakthrough for surfboard performance.

CALIFORNIA:
THE HEART OF LONGBOARDING

◆

California's post-Second World War tagline could have been 'Lighten up!' In the breathing space before Vietnam, California was about aspiration, upward mobility, lithe bodies, lemon zest, sodas and the fizz of the new. Surfing followed this fashion for levity.

IN THE 1930S AND '40s, surfboards were heavy and cumbersome and a car (a luxury) was needed to transport them to the beach, unless you had the benefit of living in front of a surf break (the ambition of every surfer). In order to really popularize and democratize surfing, boards needed to be lighter, easily handled and more readily transported. This would also encourage women, children, older people and those with disabilities to participate – making surfing inclusive. Post-war attitudes towards participation in sports, particularly in California, promoted inclusion. California was seen as a spearhead of liberation in terms of social values.

It could be argued then that the surfboard itself was an agent of democratic change within surfing. The hierarchical 'sport of kings and queens' could become the 'sport of everyone' if the board became portable and affordable – basically lighter, easier to handle and mass-produced. Some spotted the potential of new technologies to fulfil these aims. One of these was Bob Simmons – 'the man with the withered arm'.

In the mid 1930s, sixteen-year-old Bob Simmons developed a cancerous tumour in his left ankle and nearly had his leg amputated before the growth went into remission. Cycling to rehabilitate, he was hit by a car and broke his left elbow. The joint had to be fused at a 45-degree angle. While in hospital recuperating, he was advised by another patient to take up surfing to help strengthen his arm. California surfers in the mid 1940s rode lumbering and unresponsive boards, weighing almost 30 kilos (66 lbs). With his withered arm, Simmons found it impossible to carry them. He was compelled to create better equipment.

Malibu – a smooth, predictable, easy-to-ride warm summer break along a cobble point near Los Angeles – was Simmons' favourite spot, as it was with virtually all Southern Californian surfers in the 1940s and '50s. Here, the 1.9 m (6 ft 2 in) Simmons did eventually become a skilled surfer and learned the basics of designing and building surfboards.

The Simmons Board

In the late 1940s, Simmons began applying the latest ideas in mathematics and engineering to surfboard shapes and materials in his Pasadena backyard, among potted palms and orange trees. Pre-war Californian boards had been heavy redwood-balsa composites coated in varnish. Simmons decided to use balsa only (because it was lighter) and to wrap the shaped board with a layer of resin-saturated fibreglass cloth – aero-

nautics materials that would allow surfboards to become lighter and stronger. Simmons praised fibreglass (invented in Germany during the First World War) for its 'magical' properties – flexibility combined with durability.

The new Simmons board weighed about 10 kilos (22 lbs). Importantly, it was very buoyant, easily paddled and easily ridden in small surf. Surfing could gain an identity as a sport where 'all can be kings and queens'. It was typically American for the single heroic male to overcome a disability and conquer the dragon for the benefit of all – a mix of individualism, capitalist enterprise and social benefit. The American mythologist Joseph Campbell (1904–87) would later describe this archetype as 'the hero with a thousand faces'.

Velzy Hangs Ten

The chief boardmakers of the time all incorporated Simmons' design features into their own work, coating their balsa wood blanks in fibreglass and resin. In contrast to Simmons, Dale Velzy was a powerful surfer and shaper with an ego to match, a handlebar moustache and flamboyant cowboy hats. While Simmons made surfboards light, Velzy's designs made them turn easily, facilitating movement back and forth across the waveface. The overall shape of the board allowed Velzy to learn to hang ten, rolling all ten toes over the tip of the board. This was hugely significant as it would become the ultimate (but elusive) manoeuvre in longboard surfing.

The waves at Manhattan Beach were open-faced, smooth and peeling before reaching close to shore, where the ride would become tight and claustrophobic. There, they exploded onto the sand, aerated like shaken soda. It was here, in the foamy, ozone-rich shorebreak, that Velzy learned to hang ten, like a single shimmering note suspended in space, signalling the emergence of style in surfing. The trope is fascinating and again motions what America valued culturally in the aftermath of the Second World War – light, effervescent balance meets deeper danger. The oxygenation of the world was symbolized by soda consumption, the race for the conquest of space, upward mobility and the boom in light entertainment, but this, to give it edge, was rooted in stressful conquest, facing the unknown and risk (not to mention the geological instability of living on the San Andreas fault line). Extreme sports were born in this ferment, putting adrenalin, style and risk in an alchemical mix.

The New Surfing Royalty

Surfing was associated with sun-filled days, the Californian love of leisure and health, the wide, open lung of the Pacific breathing life into a post-war generation. But surfers were also outsiders, agitators, who somehow instinctively knew the rules of nature and could openly call themselves a new 'royalty' of hipsters, following what was preserved for kings and queens in Polynesia and democratizing this. One surfer

from Malibu was so light-footed that he was nicknamed 'Da Cat' – but you had better not get on the end of those claws! Miki Dora – Da Cat – was perhaps the most naturally gifted surfer of his time, but possessed an irascible temper (more red mind than blue mind). Miki Dora was the head of this dark hipster clan.

New King of the American surfers, voted 'best surfer' in the California-based *Surfer* magazine poll, was Phil Edwards. Phil was an unassuming gentle giant, a master of poise not pose, bodymindful, with an uncanny sense of balance, so that a joke emerged about Phil never falling off his surfboard. If Dora was the yang of surfing (tart, slightly bitter and hot-tempered), Edwards was the yin – expansive, welcoming and warm. Their surfing styles followed their personalities. Riding powerful waves, Phil dropped one knee to manoeuvre radically from the face to the curl – 'the drop-knee turn', soon adopted as a mark of excellence in style (and depicted on the cover of this book).

Things Bright & Beautiful

Getting back to fibreglass, that space-age industrial matter inviting its hot resin partner to harden in its weave, board design facilitated a cognitive shift, letting surfers' minds as well as bodies loose. Surfers were not just thinking, but 'being' with their new lightweight boards. And surfboards became bright and beautiful things. Polyurethane foam

replaced the wooden core. This could be moulded and colours added to laminating resins: tinted reds, bold greens, blue pin-stripes and loud block patterns, echoing the revolutions in painting initiated by the Abstract Expressionists.

The Californian revolution was complete and its new flag was that of peace and transparency based on a chemical revolution. But this flag was one of cloth transformed into shiny, hard matter in the image of the hero, the surfboard a sword. To those who see surfboards as living beings, or at least as material artefacts that engage *California's flag was* in a lively way with the humans *that of peace and* who ride them and the sea that *transparency* aims to wash them ashore, there is something of the reverse of the funeral parlour in the process of fibreglassing a surfboard. Indeed, the embalming process is coded deep in the human psyche – it is the desire to preserve not only what is dead but also what is fragile. From Neolithic burials through Egyptian embalming or mummifying to modern funeral parlour practices, there is a tradition of strengthening the fragile. The dung beetle was revered in ancient Egypt not only for its extraordinary industry but also because its carapace was a primary example of protecting the fragile interior. The same protection principle applied whether it was tarring the bottoms of wooden ships, oiling Hawaiian timber surfboards, or fibreglassing.

The Sheen of Success

Every generation looks for more advanced ways to protect what is vulnerable, whether this is covering the human skin with the latest sun creams or putting a waterproof coating on a surfboard. But this is also a metaphor for surfing. The best professional performers in any public or audience-based activity both literally and metaphorically 'coat' themselves before performance. The sociologist Erving Goffman (1922– 82) described how 'impression management' pervades our lives, seeing human interaction as a managed performance. We put on 'fronts' and 'faces' when 'frontstage', while 'back-stage' we can let our masks slip, and slip out of our costumes. All cultures have staged dramatic activities, whether religious or secular, often using elaborate masks and costumes. Profes-sional surfing too requires slipping into a role, putting on a performance, glassing oneself like a surfboard. There is a learned repertoire of moves – as if slipping into costume – and there must be ways to protect oneself against perceived public humiliation.

Part of the attraction of surfing for me, as for every surfer at the highest level of performance, was then the 'sheen' of success – the glassy surface that glows in pride of achieve-ment. Surfers are obsessed with 'glass' – the best waves, smooth and perfectly formed, are called 'glassy'. Indeed, 'glassy' and 'glossy' in surfboard design are actually what the German philosopher and economist Karl Marx (1818–83)

would call 'surplus' – unnecessary to production. Consumer society is of course obsessed with such surface gloss. While making the bottom of a surfboard glossy makes sense, to cut down on resistance, glossing the deck of a surfboard is completely unnecessary, in fact has to be compensated for by using wax to gain traction. The board is polished all over purely as an object of beauty, purely for the eye.

CORNWALL:
LAND OF THE DEAD-WHO-FEED-THE-LIVING

On those rare mornings when the sea is shrouded with vapour from a powerful new swell, the sun rising to an orchestra of skylarks, the ocean seems to spread out as a huge breakfast table with waves on the menu.

I WAS BORN INTO A COASTAL ENVIRONMENT that planted in me a feeling of freedom, self-confidence and ambition. There was no better place to grow up if you are destined to study Geography, as I was. West Cornwall (officially West Penwith) is a near-island, a massive wedge of granite, with a rugged northern edge at Zennor, a wild western wing at Land's End, and a lush and sheltered southern side around Penzance. Neolithic stone circles and quoits, Bronze Age fogous and Iron Age field systems – the classroom was right here in my backyard.

Kaolin, the white wife of Cornwall

Glistening with inclusions, clearly its conclusions

Considered and laid down, the stone-look

Of its thoughts and opinions of flowers.

FROM 'MINERALS OF CORNWALL, STONES OF CORNWALL'
PETER REDGROVE, ENGLISH POET, 1932–2003

In pursuit of the setting sun that points to the place of the dead, I learned to think of West Penwith, studded with these Neolithic burial sites, as literally a giant burial ground – a cemetery. The further west one goes, the more concentrated are the burial sites, culminating in the Isles of Scilly. This makes sense, as the sun sets here and is reborn on the opposite horizon. The dead must surely follow the sun, as it is dissolved daily only to rise elsewhere. Here, however, the Southern Californian dream of reclaiming the sun before it drops, of maintaining a permanent Hollywood smile and persona, was never going to catch on. The locals drop with the sun and suffer the consequences. Indeed, the initiation is vital. I have cherished not only the land, sea and wildlife, but also the different atmospheres, the sudden weather changes. Below West Cornwall is a radon-rich granite boss, heavily mined for tin and copper. Stripped of trees and dotted with engine houses, the collapse of tin mining offered the first post-industrial landscape in the UK. Everywhere the grey

bedrock restlessly breaks through the surface soil. It can sometimes feel intimidating. But this almost sinister appeal has been embraced by a hardy group of surfers since the 1960s. My dad, for example, travelled extensively through Europe and Australia and he and my mother married in Santa Barbara, California; but when they returned home, it was West Cornwall that had the strongest pull.

Instilling a Love of Gwenver

A devoted beach family, my parents spent countless days at West Penwith coves, especially Gwenver, with my sisters and myself. I now do the same with my children, Lola and Ruben. They love the sound of surf and the smell of salt air. Before we bound down the path to the sand, we take in the tone of the sea by sight and taste. The colours are always in flux, and you can pick out channels and associated currents by the surface differences and the lingering streamers of foam. Lola (age seven at the time of writing) is currently learning to check the whitewater gathering around the cliff edges and the distant twin-peaked island of the Brisons. She calls these 'mermaid trails': 'Look, Dad, the mermaids have left a trail.' It is also the sign of a fading swell, the same surf causing the shape of the beach to shift. There is an old shipwreck in the corner of Gwenver beach that is generally swamped in sand, but some days it bares its teeth. When I was Lola's age (in the early 1980s), it was permanently exposed.

Down at the shore where the tide has left its fingerprint, Ruben (age one at the time of writing) is discovering that the strand line is often filled with new treasures: shells, seaweed, bright jellyfish. On the beach I always feel relaxed. Once in the water, I feel like I can rest my bones in that skin of the sea for ever. I hope I can continue to share the love of the beach with my kids. I hope they learn about the changing seasons, swell patterns and tide-spills and to spot the adders in spring, the buzzards and the sea life. I hope they surf with dolphins and basking sharks. I hope they learn about the minerals in the rocks.

Recently, Lola and I were surfing tandem. She was perched at the front of my longboard, while I steered from the tail. It was spring, the days were lengthening, the gorse flickered, the heather and foxgloves blossomed and the sea was warming up. The pina colada – pineapple and coconut – smell of the gorse pervaded the air. The swallows had arrived and were dipping at speed, catching insects on the fly. It was a windy, offshore morning with a good swell running. After we missed a wave, the water blew back off the lip and we both experienced the unique secret of the 'rainbow rinse' as the spray arced over us in a private, psychedelic cave. The moment was deeply enhanced as a seal popped up and looked Lola straight in the eye.

Next summer I plan to push Ruben into his first stand-up rides at Gwenver – hopefully a ride for life.

CHAPTER FIVE

LETTING FREEDOM RING

*Mindfulness has become both
fashionable and marketable. It is, properly,
widely recommended as an alternative treatment
to drug therapies for psychological conditions such
as depression. But current approaches to mindfulness
can become mindless, ego-centred and personal.
Mindfulness can easily lead to withdrawal from the
world rather than engagement with it. I have argued
here for an ecology-centred bodymindfulness, but I will
take that even further to argue for mindfulness to move
out from self to Other, from contextualized persons
to social relations and then to politics.
Mindfulness can be radicalized.*

LIBERIA: SURF DRUMS

◆

It may seem to be simplifying things, but the 'Big Beat' around the world is still white-male-dominated and this won't do for the future. A mindful world is one in which equality and equity drive people's visions.

I WOULD ARGUE THAT PERHAPS THE WORST aspect of many recommended mindfulness exercises is that they do not recognize the difference between what the 1950s Beat Generation called 'hip' and 'square'. The best way to illustrate this is through music. Militaristic marching music, playing on the beat, is square. Jazz, inflecting around the beat and improvising, is 'hip'. Mindfulness exercises can dull by being repetitive and playing on the beat. Here's a simple way to test this. Tap out 'one-two-three-four' with your finger on a table top. Now repeat, but say 'one-AND-two-AND-three-AND-four-AND'. The 'AND' should be accentuated and fall on the upbeat as you lift your finger. If you repeat this and concentrate now on the upbeat or lifting away from the beat, you are on your first step to syncopation. It just feels so different from the militaristic downbeat. Now apply this emphasis on the upbeat to life – syncopate the everyday!

The great African American jazz drummer Max Roach (1924–2007) studied the rich drumming cultures of Africa first hand and summed up his learning in the phrase 'Let

freedom ring!' The sticks of skilled, loose drummers, as extensions of the hands, run around the kit, on fire. They form patterns, rings and polyrhythms, with tom-tom rolls accented and punctuated by snare-drum snaps. In music, there is nothing closer to surfing than drumming. But what if your drumheads are cruelly torn, your snares snapped in two, your cymbals bent, your bass pedal crushed – worse, your hands severed in torture?

Africa, the cradle of human life, has also played to a different drummer – the Lord of war and torture. After the colonial period and its terrible history of slavery and greed, when European countries withdrew from their African colonies, there was often not peaceful transition. Old tribal and ethnic rivalries were renewed, despots grabbed power and corruption set in as standard. Often, the music stopped, the beat froze, and hollowness emerged; life was desperate – entirely about survival. Between 1990 and 2004, many Liberians grew up knowing only terror, rape and hardship. Child soldiers were recruited and trained to fight in a war they did not understand, their parents already dead from the conflict.

From Darkness to Illumination

I first visited Liberia in 2006. The country had emerged from back-to-back civil wars so horrific that they reduced a flourishing city to a dark heart of terror, raining blood rather than water. Monrovia had just turned the streetlights on for the

first time in fifteen years. 'It symbolizes our journey from darkness to illumination,' announced President Ellen Johnson Sirleaf, Africa's first elected (and widely celebrated) female head of state.

When I returned just before the Ebola outbreak of 2014, the bullet holes had been plastered over, wounds healed, and the street signs were now selling capitalism, the markets buzzing. Where a generation was lost to education, the chief billboard message was 'Go to school'. Kids were back in classrooms and once low, boiling black skies had split open to reveal what was hidden by war – the light of liberty.

Atlantic waves rise like black-bodied whales

Travelling with a Liberian friend called Dominic Johns, I wanted to find out how the country had changed since 2006 and to ask if surf tourism had any place in that regeneration. Establishment of a local surf culture may be one of the most promising things to have happened to Robertsport, close to the border with Sierra Leone, where Atlantic waves rise like black-bodied whales, showing sharp white backbones, unravelling in cadence along the beachfront.

The coast here is shaped like a clenched fist, rocky head-lands like knuckles defining surf breaks packed with promise. We parked under the towering 200-year-old cotton silk tree where Dominic and Liberia's pioneer Scottish surfer and aid worker Magnus Wolfe Murray own a camping pitch. Dominic

inspected his land and greeted local friends with the national handshake. The grab-clasp-finger-click is a snappy celebration of freedom because it requires an intact finger (not cut off and lost by warlords or slave masters).

The Robertsport Crew

I paddled out to meet a handful of locals. The Robertsport crew has developed beautifully spontaneous surfing styles as they adapt to the local ecology. Some are graceful and unshowy; a few are intricate, crab-like, shifting sideways on slippery faces and ramping up as the wind clears off the foam; while others are gung-ho, climbing and dropping like skateboarders on uncertain ramps, loving the unexpected shapes that peak up like surfacing sea life to grab you.

I recognized Morris Gross. He was just nine when I was last here (in 2006), thunderstruck by surfing: 'I wanna ride, let me ride your board,' he said. He quickly learned on the whitewater waves. It got under his skin. Only another ride could satisfy the itch. I knew that those intoxicating first rides would grip him tightly and take him places – mentally and physically – he never knew existed. Morris begged me to take him home with me to Cornwall for one week of schooling. 'You can learn a lot right here,' I said. 'This place needs you to look after it. Education that is also sensitive to cultural tradition is key to the future.' Morris was beginning to understand the intrinsic value of Robertsport's natural resources.

Morris was now seventeen and a brilliant surfer. He paddled into the next wave, dropped, and drove down the point, climbing and falling, then skimming over a series of unfolding lips, as close to flying as wave-riding will take you. Next set. My wave. Take off, climb, arc, skip, then catapult ahead and finally land on the sand. We walked back up the point together, laughing.

'Great to see that you have turned into such a good surfer, Morris.'

'But it's school I love best.'

'What subjects?'

'Mathematics and physics. I want to study engineering at university, and apply it to surfboard design.'

I quietly punched the air as we paddled back out, pleased to learn that Morris was on the right trajectory, mixing surf and turf – growing muscle but letting the mind graze.

There is now a dedicated crew of about thirty local surfers, sharing around ten boards. Central to the development of this local scene are two young Californian surfers – Sean Brody and Daniel Hopkins. They wanted to bring friendship, help and genuine investment to the village and launched the Kwepunha Surf Retreat. They also run an eagerly awaited Liberians-only annual surf competition and manage various health care and community programmes. These priceless waves have offered a wonderful, self-replenishing commodity – that of sustainable surf tourism.

SIERRA LEONE: THE ANIMAL PULSE

◆

Two or three times a year I travel with an international adventure team called surfEXPLORE to find and document new surfing waves. We are committed to ecologically sensitive and culture-sensitive projects, often in post-conflict zones such as Sierra Leone.

FROM WORKING IN OTHER AREAS of post-conflict Africa I have learned never to stereotype places through the frames of their wars, or limit expectations or understandings according to media representations – in Sierra Leone's case, accounts of the generations who abandoned farming to sieve dirt in stagnant muddy waters, bent over in aching heat, mining blood diamonds in the hope of a winner; and child soldiers high on a deadly cocktail of cocaine and gunpowder known as *brown-brown*. But as nations reflect on the scar tissue from wars, these mindless (as opposed to mindful) images can offer misrepresentations of future possibilities, often immobilizing creative change, inviting forms of piety and aid to places that demand instead ecological education – how to learn sustainability and self-sufficiency.

◆

It is not down on any map; true places never are.

FROM 'MOBY-DICK'
HERMAN MELVILLE, AMERICAN NOVELIST, 1819–91

◆

We plan our trips mindfully not hastily, using online resources such as Google Earth wisely and always working with local contacts. We did not go to Sierra Leone to echo the newsreels and offer pieties, but to use surfing to get under the skin of the coastline and showcase her potential, as a new facet of the emerging diamond that is a politically and eco-logically stable nation. This is mindful surf travel in action. Of course, water, electricity and available work are front-line issues for the population (and most recently the Ebola out-break), but this country is ambitious and on the rise.

Afrobeat

Local music is a great metaphor for Sierra Leone's resur-gence. This celebration of life is perhaps best captured in Freetown's music heroes Ansumana Bangura, S.E. Rogie and Abdul Tee-Jay. They gained global recognition before the civil war for fusing drumming templates and traditional songs with Afrobeat guitars and calypso styles. They called it 'palm-wine' music, then 'Milo-jazz' after the empty Milo cans filled with stones that are used as rattles. Recently the Sierra Leone Refugee All Stars have put the nation's rich musical heritage and innovations back on the map, blending call-and-response, palm-wine and reggae, and packing out concert venues. These are once-exiled men whose joyful beat was born in unimagi-nable turmoil during the civil war in refugee camps in Guinea. Today the soundtrack to the dance floors of Freetown is hip-

hop and dancehall, using keyboards and digital mixers. But beach parties still blast out the palm-wine 'oldies'.

Ragged *poda poda* mini taxis rule the streets in the vibrant capital Freetown, blasting the latest hits from booming speakers. Loudhailers encourage tax payment, while musicians satirically wear their tax bills and sing about lack of water and light. Hair salons are crammed full, selling wigs and performing intricate cuts. The old Krio clapboard houses are coloured russet red and black. The spoken Krio is equally stylish, once a phonetic trading slang for freed slaves – West Indian soldiers who fought for the British against the French between 1793 and 1815, settled and assimilated into the local communities. Now it is a full-blown language peppered with West African greetings, such as the ubiquitous:

'*Aw di bohdi?*' (How is the body / How are you doing?)

'*Di bohdi wehl*' (The body is well / Good, thanks!)

The dry season was fast drying up and we caught the very tail end, surfing south from Freetown along the western Peninsula. Uniform blue waves met mountains that rose from the coast like giant beasts – *Serra Lyoa* means *Lion Mountains* in Portuguese, the dominant language of early European exploration of West Africa. Wide open creeks dotted with bright working fishing boats cut through the coast, forming long, easy-to-ride waves. There was a constant sound of cicadas and, on the weekends, infectious guitar-based music poured out from Krio wooden-board houses.

> ## Bureh Beach Surf Club
>
> One of the most exciting things happening along Sierra Leone's 400 kilometres (250 miles) of mainland coast is the development of the Bureh Beach Surf Club. *Di waves dem go mak u feel fine* is the club motto. This is positive eco-tourism in action because the scene is growing slowly and humbly with the local community at the helm. There is a clubhouse, kitchen café and camp pitch. Surf lessons are in place and soon there will be accommodation. Perhaps lifeguarding will follow, especially for the busloads travelling to the coast from Freetown for beach parties every weekend. Like neighbouring Liberia, Sierra Leone is developing a proud local surf culture and beginning to attract surf travellers. Our surfEXPLORE group donated a surfboard to the club, which is soon to host an international competition. Bureh Beach could be a bright flame for African surf tourism, but it needs more oxygen to keep the fire alight.

At Cockle Point, on the south side of River Number Two, we stayed in a new guesthouse complex of cottages shaded by stubby mango trees. Fast-paced football games pitted and patterned the beach. The local sand-bottom surf break peeled majestically for 50 metres (just over 50 yards). The backdrop was just as mouthwatering: a dense mangrove, red-flowered

locust beans, then hills of ironwood and the occasional tower-
ing cotton tree. The waves were completely empty and, for
better or worse, we brought the inscription of surfing, perhaps putting smiles on their faces.

Exploring the Turtle Islands

If exploration is the act of searching to discover new information
and practices, rather than the colonial project of exploiting
resources, the 'exploration' part of the trip (we had been
planning for over a year) was to explore the remote Turtle
Islands in the south of the country. As far as we know, we are
the first to surf (and document the surfing) in this archipel-
ago, a web of animist secret societies, surrounded by shallow
shifting sandbars. We thrive on this notion of surfing the clean
slate. It is not a conquering thing, but a traveller's – or, better,
explorer's – delight.

There are nine islands spread across 60 km (40 miles) pop-
ulated by approximately 1,000 people living in self-sufficient
fishing communities, specializing in net-fishing, mat-making
and weaving. We stayed with Henri Pelissier, who runs a small
eco-lodge and campsite called Turtle Dream on the island of
Bakie. Henri has gained privileged access to the local community – he adopted and raised the island chief's son Abu
when his mother died during childbirth. Abu is now in his
early twenties and works with Henri and a cast of other Bakie
locals to cater for a potential new wave of adventure tourists.

We set up a rhythm – surfing each morning around the Turtle Islands, eating a fish lunch at the camp and in the afternoon exploring surf breaks marked on our maps. Fishermen worked alone in dugout canoes at dawn, then by midday in groups casting nets across the shore in sync with the tide. The marine and bird life considerably outnumbered the human. In just one afternoon I spotted black kites, terns, kingfishers, eagles and schools of barracudas and tarpon. Fired up on the sea life, we met the peaking swell, hawk-eyed. Long, overhead waves beat the sand like drummers, air pockets swelling the whitewater and showering us in salt spray.

The Drums Take Over
In the mid summer of 2014 the Ebola outbreak escalated, crippling tourism in Sierra Leone. Like neighbouring Liberia, as Ebola stabilizes, surfers will be some of the first adventure travellers to the return to this shore, drumming the animal pulse to align mind, body and spirit.

But what is this animal pulse? My reading of mindfulness as a bodymindfulness is to recover the instinct of reflexivity-within-action. Instinct is often described as 'blind' or thoughtless. An animal reflex, however, as every martial artist knows, is not at all blind, but sharply focused. Mindfulness is a within-body reflection as well as a within-mind reflection. If we take the many forms of African drumming as an example, at first the drummer is conscious of his or her actions and plays

on or around the beat as if slightly detached, feeling a way into the music. As the music progresses, however, the drums overtake the drummer or the sticks begin to play the drummer. The drums are played by instinct and we know this because new improvised patterns appear that surprise the drummer as much as the audience.

HAITIAN VODOU

The Caribbean nation of Haiti was born not just in a slave revolt in 1804 (the only successful one in history), but in revulsion at the idea that one person can enslave another. But how do you befriend an 'Other' culture?

HAITI (the western side of the island of Hispaniola) is shaped like a crab's claws waiting to snap. Undoubtedly, Haiti will get purchase on you. So how do you get purchase on Haiti as a surfer? Exploring the coastline is a starting point. But Haiti may also snap at your fingers. It does not want to be fingered by outsiders, yet is permanently subject to this fingering. Haiti must be imagined literally – geographically, historically and politically – before surfing its coastline, and it must also be de-literalized and reconfigured through a literary or poetic imagination. It must be re-searched, experienced and lived in body and imagination. In particular, its Vodou tradition may impact upon the visitor, perhaps stripping back

the skin and allowing the skeleton to walk out for a brief period, convene with the dead and then slip back under the skin as a refreshed frame. This in-and-out-of-body experience is also a mode of enquiry that can be part of mindful travel.

In Haiti, the curtain is always half-raised, so that you never know if the show is about to begin or has just ended, but you had better be on the right side of the curtain. The *rah-rah* drumbeat and *tom-tom* roll is always there, in the background, rattling the soul. You cannot afford to be weak in spirit here, or mean of heart. Haitian spirits say: We will never double-cross you as long as you keep the faith of this strange double-cross world.

The Blood Pulse of Port au Prince

Out of the plane window on a clear day you notice that Haiti's outline looks more like a caricature of a human heart than a crab's claw, blood supply flowing right into Port au Prince. In the capital something rough, resilient, ironic and brave persists – a Creole wit, grace, artistic energy, a poignant religious expressiveness in Vodou and a nervous edge of risk-taking. This is the blood pulse of Haiti, inspiring passion. It is a love-like experience, unpredictable, unmissable. And you know that when you get home you will be struck by an outpouring of emotion, missing it badly. The weather of places, their atmospheres, their pressures, will seep into your psyche and inhabit your being. Every time I visit Haiti I feel like I am

The Goddess of the Marketplace

Port au Prince boils with traffic, the ubiquitous *taptap* pick-ups with backs raised, carrying people on benches, some so loaded with products that they grind the ground, releasing sparks, maybe giving more purpose to their missions. Street vendors jump off and within minutes lay out a spectrum of biscuits, sodas, cigarettes, soaps, perfumes and second-hand clothes. People are setting up, bartering, eating, arguing, all for *Ayizan* – the goddess of the marketplace. Women dressed in radiant tops, radiating style, carry heavily loaded banana trays on their heads and set up shop, berating their husbands and lovers, gossiping with fellow street vendors and spreading news by *tele djol* – word of mouth. Baskets also do the talking, overfilled with mangoes, plantains, figs, breadfruit, cashews, meat-packed pastries and dried fish. In this setting, it is hard to confirm the description that 'Haiti is one of the poorest places on the planet'.

wearing my skeleton on the outside of my body and that my nervous system is stretched over that. I am infected by stored trauma from a certain kind of raw exposure to this country and its soul. I feel that country's history impress me with a force that leaves me reeling. I can only deal with that through mindful surf travel.

Carnival Characters

Recently I visited the art-capital Jacmel on the south coast to experience carnival. On the outskirts of town there was a rising hubbub of distant noise. I was stopped by 'rope throwers' – *lans kod* – eight menacing figures blocking the road. They were covered in charcoal and sugar cane syrup, making a pitch-black, sticky skin. They brandished maracas, rattles and a range of percussion instruments. An audience gathered. Through a heavily stylized song and dance routine, the rope throwers mocked the masters of their colonial past and celebrated independence through sly civility.

The colour of carnival is predominantly orange, a searing sun. Snaking through the crowd was a line of men sporting prominent buck teeth, red jackets with yellow trims, black hats, silver coins and trousers with pin lines. They were Chaloskas, mocking corrupt General Charles Oscar, who terrorized Jacmel in the early 1900s. Long-haired Master Richard bought justice from his suitcase bulging with money, while hunchback Dr Calypso cracked a whip and set out to scare children. Small boys in green leotards kicked up dust as they hopped, hidden under shells of papier-mâché and imitating frogs – *crapo*. Birds, bushes and trees followed Kongo and Arawak Indians and giant butterflies. Madame Lasiren, the mermaid, walked with her children. Vodou honours hundreds of *lwa* – gods, spirits and natural forces – recognizing all life in a full democracy of beings.

Surfing as Dance

As part of the carnival procession, Fosaj, a local dance troupe, accompanied papier-mâché puppeteers to a driving drum-based music. I'm not a musician. But I see the shape of moving water as a blank canvas to perform wailing music against peeling waves. Translucent walls and transparent peaks make sense of surfing's marriage with music and the code that this unlocks. Surfers are wave musicians, improvising against the orchestra of the grinding sea, concentrating on intense, short solos and raucous codas. But surfing can also be considered a form of dance.

The lead Fosaj dancer set the pace and the other dancers followed, appearing to skate across the ground as the drumming became sharp and unforgiving. The dancers repeated the basic trope of throwing off the shackles of slavery in apparent rage, violence and delirium, but with a core of elegance, precision and pride. The lead dancer acted as houngan – a male priest in Haitian Vodou – in a part choreographed, part improvised ceremony. He swayed, then swung side to side, like a building swell, the whole group moving forward as a set of waves, arms now splayed, leaving the rolling ocean like ascending seabirds, the dance looking to me like a mirror of surfing. I became lost in the parallel sensations of surfing as dance: the long arc of a noseride, feet sliding back and forth like footwork on a board, quick, improvised direction changes, flow in the face of swirling waters.

The dancers were now as one, feet rising, jumping in unison, the drummers like sets of crashing waves. The dancers gained momentum, following the ever-rising cross-beats of the drummers. The solos were intense and set against the fabric of drumbeats that resembled a grinding sea with relentless forward motion bent on making sand out of rock. The dancing was raucous, knees and hips gyrating, elbows out, wrists rolling like fishermen casting nets. The drum work moved back and forth from the skeins to cracking rimshots like thunderheads.

The dancers followed the ever-rising cross-beats of the drummers

As the energy intensified, blood pumping harder, heart rates soaring, the dancers mimicked being mounted by the divine horseman in Vodou. The *lwa*, the Haitian spirit that the ceremony had invoked, had arrived. The dancers had become horses to the spirit rider. In Vodou, the pillar of a community is the houngan or mambo (female priest). But Vodou is a democratic faith. Each believer not only has direct contact with the spirits, but also receives them into his or her body, quite literally dancing to become a god. The function of Vodou is to serve the gods as natural forces, to reconcile, celebrate and share. Under the guidance of the houngan, the lead dancer (as god) rode the dancers as a herd, but rider god and human horse were one as possession took hold and the current of the celebration moved through them as one body.

Jeter le Masque

The distinguishing feature of the carnival ritual is *déguisement* – a masking that is an unmasking. There is a story behind every mask, following the French expression *jeter le masque* – to show one's true colours. To surf you must also let go, to risk yourself in the unpredictable moment of the breaking wave. I think of surfing as a type of carnival in which the procession is regular sets of waves breaking irregularly, often loosely, seeming to seek out the best way to trip you or catch you unawares. Surfers must inhabit a thin line between fish and bird at the ocean's skin, and bust out their carnival moves as the thunder of sets rolls by.

Surfing with Chachou

As the carnival passed by, at Pistons in Jacmel, the waves were peeling like a steam train. Pistons is where surfing started in Haiti, on a long wave by a wrecked boat (all that is left is a big piston). I joined local surfer Chachou. Outback the sea was a big sweep of blues at the purple end of the spectrum, bruised by deep currents. On the inside was a band of green as the waves raked the rocks. Chachou and I swung into the sets, kissing the waves' lips to show intimacy, turning sharply from the tail to map the geography and disappearing down the line in imitation of the train ride that was the breaking wave itself.

The rides were like trading jokes – a slow build-up finishing in a sharp punch line and a splatter of laughter. Chachou waited for a set perched like a crane fishing on the reef, a perfect model for patience. At the right moment he pounced – timing is everything – reading the refraction of the wave, taking off and then improvising as if straight into a solo. The surf re-stimulated our senses, only to remind us that at the tideline the water tasted foul – it was polluted.

The ocean's magnificent carnival of drumming waves had a disappointing coda, as if mystery and invention suddenly expired where sea and beach kiss. We trod our way gingerly onto the beach, which was littered with a virtual ocean of green plastic bottles. Despite the pre-carnival beach clean, overnight the beach had been covered again in plastic bottles from the Grande Rivière de Jacmel, which flows onto the sand, bringing boulders and sculpting the surf break. But there is no reason why these plastic bottles cannot have value – local kids could clear them up and sell them for recycling. The river that brings these bottles onto the beach should be cleaned further up its reach. Chachou understands these environmental paradoxes and his interaction with this beach has given him a particular perspective on the coastscape. The sea is Chachou's workshop as fisherman, lifeguard and surfer, and the bridge of sand is the daily portal to each of these crafts and arts. He knows better than anybody that for Jacmel to grow as a market of cultural tourism, it must clean up its act.

MINDFULNESS EXERCISE

VISUALIZING THE RIDE

Surfers have to move from lying down prone to standing up in the blink of an eye. Visualize lying prone on the board and popping up in one clean movement. This now becomes an exercise of balance. Concentrate on your open palms – a secret to balance in the surf, riding the board. Visualize yourself standing, knees flexed, feet shoulder-width apart, back straight, arms an aid to balance. Surfboards are actually turned (a direction change) by looking where you want to go, rotating the upper body in that direction, and applying pressure to the relevant side of the back foot. Twist from the waist. Arms help lift your torso. This posture of course requires core strength and timing, but again this can be visualized.

When you are at the coastline, remember that image of lying to standing up in one clean sweep, and translate it to the take-off. Strangely, this exercise will also help you to paddle for longer, and catch more waves, because visualizing yourself riding the waves, popping up in one movement, is a vital step in preparing perception and bodily movement.

It is a mistake to think that surfing demands just practice, fitness and strength. Visualization is just as important. Before surfing competitions I visualize the ride, before a surf I visualize the experience – in fact, I even visualized winning my first European surfing title in Portugal in 1999.

Summary

When Xenophon describes the military adventure of *anabasis* (a movement from the coast to the interior), no step is taken without preparation. Visualize before you act. You can paddle out, catch and surf a wave in your mind's eye, but the secret is to not stay in the mind's eye, but to visualize a whole bodily change in muscular tone.

CHAPTER SIX

BECOMING CHILDREN OF THE TIDE

*Surfing in Chinese — chong lang —
literally means 'entering the waves'. Not taking
them over, or dominating them, but entering into their
collective spirit and surfing as the wave guides. The
Chinese Taoist tradition suggests to watch for nature's
pulses and currents and to follow them, to go with the
flow. To enter the Tao of surfing, you need dedication,
a really good eye and a feel for the wave — to follow
the pulse and improvise with its patterns and
paradoxes. This is what a handful of surfers have
been doing from Hong Kong to Hainan Island
over the last decade.*

THE TAO OF SURFING

◆

Ninth-century Chinese alchemists discovered gunpowder while seeking the elixir of life. This led to the invention of fireworks, a spectacular celebration of life. The sages knew the secret mystery to life is making something of it, through effort and mindful attention.

RIGHT NOW IN HAINAN (a subtropical island off southern China) it feels like surfing has begun its life in the country that is ready to explode over the next decade, but its trajectory is uncertain. What is certain is that the provincial government of Hainan is investing wholeheartedly in surfing to establish a new trajectory. A surf break called Riyue Wan (Sun Moon Bay) hosts the annual Women's and Men's World Longboard Championships, and the river bore wave known as the 'Silver Dragon' breaking down the Qiantang River on the mainland holds an annual competition. This is arguably the longest wave in the world. The gunpowder trail has been ignited and the dragon is stirring. The sages knew that the mystery to life is not in the virgin firework, but in its lighting, as the sparks of mindful attention fly. And, by carefully following the pulse, you will almost certainly, say the sages, discover the unexpected.

But a quest to reclaim China's surfing heritage is just beginning, led by an Italian expat and surf historian called Nik Zanella, who lives on Hainan. 'My fascination with Chinese waves started before I even got to Hainan,' explains Nik, 'and it was when I was studying a degree in Chinese at university in Venice in the late 1980s. I started finding traces of water and ocean in Chinese philosophy, especially Taoism. In the *Tao Te Ching* water is synonymous with flow and the most powerful of the elements.'

Qiongzhu's Surfing Buddhas

Following countless surf trips exploring the coastline of China for waves, Nik moved to Hainan in 2010 and became central to the growing surf scene, teaching, writing, working at competitions and coaching the national surf team. Nik continues, 'I spend a lot of time on the ocean, so in 2011 I took a trip from Hainan inland to Yunnan, which is a lush green forest area, a bamboo grove, with a lot of ethnic minorities in the south-west of China. I went to the Qiongzhu Temple near Kunming, 600 kilometres (370 miles) from the coast. I walked into this temple and saw a full wall of surfing Buddhas. My jaw dropped. There is a green wave and thirty surfing Buddhas carved along the walls of the hall.'

Nik discovered that after the temple was rebuilt in the 1880s following a fire, an emperor commissioned a local artist to carve 500 life-sized statues of *luohans* (Buddhist arhats, or 'enlightened ones'). Two full walls are dedicated to the act of *chong lang* with men of all ages depicted riding a green overhead wave.

'That sparked something in my mind,' Nik continues, 'so I started researching Chinese poetry to see if I could find ancient traces of surfing. There's a famous compilation called *300 Tang Poems* from the eighth century. I searched not only for the Chinese words for "wave", but also for "tide", because "tide" was almost synonymous with "wave" in Chinese traditional culture. The first traces that I found are from Sichuan written into a poem about a lady complaining about her husband leaving her alone to go back to the village and trade, and disregarding her sexual needs. She concluded: *Had I known the tides are so reliable, I would have married a surfer.* The traditional word for surfer was *nong chao er* – "children of the tide".

'Once I found the words "children of the tide", I discovered further evidence coming from the thirteenth century in an article called "Watching the tide", accompanied by manuals describing the construction of hollow bamboo surfboards used to ride river bore waves in extravagant festivals attended by thousands of people and various dignitaries. The translation describes the tides from the fifteenth to the eighteenth day of the eighth moon, coming out of the horizon as loud as thunder, exploding and rising up, with hundreds of brave watermen riding river waves the size of whales on wooden boards, springing up, and performing manoeuvres.'

> *Coming out of the horizon*
> *as loud as thunder*

According to Nik's research, river surfing festivals in ancient China were already a lesson in Tao. They took an equal mix of organization and improvisation – the light fizz of pretty sparklers and the crackle of jumping jacks. Perhaps Taoism, Confucianism and Buddhism were being brought together in a syncretic appreciation of nature, suggesting that if you respect the wave you get the best out of the ride.

The Balance of Forces

I have travelled to Hainan to surf and explore the coastline for waves at least ten times since 2003. Above all I have discovered that China is a culinary culture. Taste and smell to the Chinese are just as important as looking and touching. Here, you do not just think the philosophy of Tao, the balance of forces, but you taste it through pure, clean, contrasting flavours. The French scholar of Chinese aesthetics, François Jullien, argues that Westerners want to eat life, consume it, with an imperative to control in the instant, where the Chinese tradition of 'vital nourishment' is to tend life over time, rather than consume it now.

While the Cultural Revolution changed much in China, the principle of vital nourishment remains sacred. This is literally exhibited in the way that a Chinese family will feed you with obvious pleasure, as a freely given gift, not in any way demanding that you have an obligation to return the gift. The family glances off you so that you feel honoured rather than

obligated. I now see 'vital nourishment' as a core aesthetic practice in China – a means of subtly coming at an issue from several points of view to bring out the barely perceptible, a distinct but underplayed flavour. Contrast this with the urgent need for Westerners to get to the point. It strikes me that I have been living this Chinese way all my surfing life, where I have always practised surfing as subtle inflection, indirection, small but telling shifts in weight distribution producing big effects on the wave face. Longboard surfing is all about cat-like agility and lifting off, not bringing down your weight full force or pushing against the unfolding, natural movement of the wave. Surely such glancing off rather than blundering in is a key element of mindfulness, an attitude and a posture for life.

TAUGHT BY NATURE

◆

While China has been overhauled politically through Mao's Cultural Revolution, in its spiritual heart it remains an idiosyncratic mix of conservative Confucianist manners and wild Taoist invention and verve, which the American poet Wallace Stevens described as presence, not force.

To BE CHINESE IS TO BELONG to the oldest civilization on earth, continuous for twenty-five centuries. Today, three forces meet in China: a compelling urge for modernization –

Chinese Thought in the Western Soul

The more I visit Hainan, the more I feel that Chinese thought is already embedded somewhere in the soul of the West and that the proclaimed division between Occident and Orient is not so strong. While Westerners live with the heliocentric revolution of Copernicus and Kepler, nobody thinks of the earth circling the sun when we watch a sunrise or sunset. Rather, you are awash with the glory of it all. As you wipeout on a solid whitewater wave, self-survival may be at the centre of your immediate cosmos, but how can you not at the same time be in awe of the churning wave and its impactful poetry? François Jullien puts it simply and elegantly – to appreciate Chinese interactions, especially the importance of glancing off something rather than going at it directly, the Westerner must slow down his or her thought. Indeed, studies tracking eye movements in ordinary perception or 'looking' tell you that, most of the time, Westerners are 'glancing' also, taking things in holistically, looking sideways. 'Eye contact' would be very challenging – most of the time that we gaze on another person's face, we look at the mouth, not the eyes, dampening down the direct, penetrating gaze for the off-centre, the offbeat. Paradoxically, it is the sideways glance that sums up the presence of another or assesses character and not the penetrating gaze in whose presence the other may wither.

mixed with tradition (or the reinvention of tradition), and the still powerful grip of state socialism. But I would argue that Confucianism and Taoism remain in dialogue even within state socialism. Confucianism is about the polite and obedient citizen; Taoism is about a return to the rhythms and presences of nature, typified by the wild 'mountain man' in solitary retreat and contemplation. For decades, Maoist authorities derided both traditions as feudal superstition, but it seems that Taoism and Confucianism are indelibly imprinted on the population, as complementary expressions of the raw and the cooked, nature and culture.

Confucius suggested that perfect balance is reflected in calm water, a model for composure. This is the social instinct – polite compromise. At the heart of Taoism is a paradoxical wild calm. Nature is a vortex and you are at its eye, involved but not involved. We are back to the twin essences of surfing, the tuberide and the noseride: both require absolute poise, calm and a kind of withdrawal at the eye of the vortex.

The Way of Power

The *Tao Te Ching* – The Way of Power – is a free-spirited collection of the sayings by Lao Tzu, a supposed contemporary of Confucius (known as Kongzi in China). Tao is the natural flow of the cosmos, and nature follows the Tao. Humans, with their conscious wills, go against the Tao. The goal of the sage is to harmonize with the Tao and become one with nature.

Lao Tzu wrote: 'In his every movement a man (or woman) of great virtue follows the Way and the Way only.' The practice of Taoism involves balancing opposites (yin and yang) as they move into each other, a philosophy many surfers can relate to as they deal with a constantly changing environment. Indeed, Lao Tzu was enchanted by water: 'Under heaven nothing is more soft and yielding than water. Yet for attacking the solid and strong, nothing is better; it has no equal.'

Taoism is clearly a template for surfing to the emerging Hainan surfers: the yin and yang in revolution, a still centre. A strange balance between Confucianism, Taoism and Buddhism yields San Jiao He Yi – Three Teachings flowing into one – again suggesting that if you respect the wave, you get the best out of the ride.

Learning by Immersion

Monica Guo and Darci Liu are two Chinese surfers at the heart of the emerging culture in Hainan. Fostering a deep love for the ocean, they actively raise awareness in their coastal communities through teaching surfing, volunteering and helping to protect endangered ocean animals, such as sea turtles. When Darci, a former ballerina, moved to Sanya, in southern Hainan, with her Californian husband, she had to learn to swim at the same time as she was learning to surf. That learning by immersion, combined with her natural athletic ability as a dancer, translated perfectly into the skills

needed to become a great surfer (and the first female surfer in Hainan). I asked Darci what advice she would give to young Chinese surfers starting out:

'I think follow the right route. Do the right thing, ride the right waves. It's not just pick up a board, paddle in, stand up and catch a wave and today I'm a surfer. No. I think start from the beginning and get into the ride. It's also about respecting other surfers. That's how I want to see the rest of the Chinese surfers grow, to get the respect from all over the world.'

Monica Guo grew up in Yangshuo, Guilin, famed for the Li River and the striking karst topography, which attracts the world's best rock climbers. Working as an adventure guide, Monica travelled to Sanya (the beach tourism capital of Hainan) and became captivated by surfing because of the calm the activity produced within her. Monica moved to Sanya and started a girls' surf camp, where she invites young Chinese surfers to enjoy the ocean safely. Monica talks eloquently about the dance of surfing, and when I asked her what it feels like when she cross-steps and noserides on a fast wave, she replied: 'I feel like a dolphin, playing in the waves. And I also feel like a bird, because I'm high up, on top of the nose. I feel free. I have nothing else on my mind: just me, the waves and my board. This is how beautiful it is. It's really beautiful.'

Justin Tiller, another Chinese surfer and close friend of Monica and Darci, explains: 'Surfing has changed my life, and since I started I like to protect the ocean. I think the ocean is my home. If more people get involved in surfing in China, they probably want to save the ocean as I do. I think this is going to be good for everybody.'

It is possible that the Chinese will eventually produce a world surfing champion and establish surfing with a very strong team ethic. The Taoist way is to have a hawk eye for opportunity and then to follow its flow – as if water breaking a dam could then become a wave of opportunity. Here then is a lesson for mindfulness – develop that hawk eye for opportunity, recognize the seed, judge the potential and enrol. But this opportunism must also have an ethical dimension. Judge also what may be the effects of the emerging venture on the lives of others and the health of the planet.

BUDDHISM: THE STILL
POINT AT THE CENTRE OF MOVEMENT

If I understand Buddhism correctly, living fully in the present in a sense eradicates time, for there is no mindless wandering to recollection and no fruitless future guesswork. This state of mind is when you perform at your best, mindful of the now.

ONE OF THE SEMINAL BOOKS of the hippy era, published in 1971, is Baba Ram Dass' *Be Here Now*. Ram Dass was once Dr Richard Alpert, a psychologist at Harvard who was central to the first wave of serious research into the effects of LSD. Ram Dass gave up all drug-related paths for a Western-oriented Buddhism where spirituality and psychology freely mixed. Central to his teaching is the ancient Zen Buddhist notion of 'suchness'. Many people imagine that Buddhist meditation and mindfulness is a switching off from life's distractions, but 'suchness' teaches the opposite – to accept nature just as it appears: as famous Zen koans say, to hear the 'plop!' of the frog as it hits the water; to note the exact bend of a tree as it resists the wind. But, and this is a big but, 'suchness' does not teach that we should just accept life. Far from it – the exact hysterical pitch of a bigot's voice berating someone in a moment of prejudice is to closely notice; but this does not mean that you simply stop at closely noticing. Indeed, the close noticing makes you even more aware of the bigotry and then more determined to challenge these views.

Zen Buddhism takes you to the red-hot heart of an object, an idea or a feeling, and then reduces it through a swift switch to intense contemplation. This is caught in Zen koans – parables that burn with penetrating description and finish on a cool note of contemplation. Soyen Shaku, the Zen teacher who first brought Zen Buddhism to America, where Beat poets such as Allen Ginsberg and Gary Snyder eagerly adopted the teachings and practices, said: 'My heart burns like fire but my eyes are as cold as dead ashes.' Experience ignites but a subsequent contemplation creates reflective distance.

Now Is The Time

Staying in the present is one of the most important things when surfing. Paradoxically, planning a surf means thinking ahead the whole time, as you spend a lot of time putting together clues as to where the best breaks may be. But within this general frame of preparedness, the rule is to stick with the now. Jazz music can teach so much about this. The joke runs: 'What is the time?' The response: '*Now* is the time'! Those who make improvisation in the present look easy are thinking ahead, but confidently drawing this knowledge into the here and now (or 'hear'-AND-now).

Staying in the Present

When I first visited Hainan in 2003, I travelled with a great friend, surfEXPLORE photographer John Callahan, to the north-east of the island. Scouting the horizon, searching for the consistent waves, suddenly our senses were magnetized by some greater force, turning us landward from the azure sea, where a huge golden Buddha, elevated on a pyramid of steps, sat watching us, watching the surf, contemplating existence. We climbed to the ancient Gautama, juniper smoke rising from a shrine scattered with incense sticks and jade. It was a powerful moment, the presence of this 1,600-year-old survivor from the Tang Dynasty, the Mahajana School, a lost piece of China's history, made all the more powerful by the fact that the Maoist Revolution had attempted to eradicate the Buddhist legacy.

The Buddha reminded me of the folly of our ways, always anticipating, always wondering what is around the next headland and failing to live in the present. The Dharma (the way of acceptance) is the way to nirvana. You do not search for nirvana as we were searching for waves; you live it as the present. The surf instantly became more appealing. Here we were, surfers in China, pursuing our dreams in a country trying to modernize and reinvent itself. But there was a paradox.

> *You do not search for nirvana; you live it as the present*

The legacy of the Maoist regime is a disjunction between past and present and Marxism is all about historical determinism, society evolving with a strong sense of history. Yet Chairman Mao erased history to enforce the present, deliberately destroying China's antiquity, where the Red Guard attempted to erase Buddhism and its Tibetan stronghold. But here, on the periphery, there remained a striking vestige of the past that ironically taught the value of staying in the present.

A Spiritual Rinse

Surfing for me is a 'spiritual rinse'. And there is no better place for surfing in the present than Asia. Throughout various surf trips across the continent I have learned something very important about being mindful. It chimes with the overall theme that I argue for in this book – that mindfulness is not a practice of going in to self or ego, but one of recognizing what the world affords and tuning to this – inside-out rather than outside-in, or bodymindful.

In Asia, if you stay in self and ego, your nerves will frazzle. Your body is stripped of privacy and your sense of self dissolves in the clamour of life. Leave your nerves exposed and life is unbearable. Rather, you must connect out to the bigger bodymind of the community, to an extended and shared cognition. What is tough to get at first is that the new collective thinking is characterized by its contradictions. Once you get the hang of hanging out with this collective emotional mind, staying in the present is easier. It is just like surfing waves in a crowd. Think 'flock', 'pattern' and 'tribe' and let the 'I' dissolve in the 'we'. Now I am sounding like Baba Ram Dass, but I am sure you get the picture. After all, Ram Dass himself said: 'If you don't get the picture, change channels!'

MINDFULNESS EXERCISE

WAXING UP

Good-quality surfing conditions often lead to crowds. This can be frustrating because it is harder to catch a wave, you often feel you are getting in the way of others and sometimes others get in your way. A solution is surfing on wind-blown days, when it is less crowded; in the wintertime, when shops and local services are closed; or early or late, when it's less crowded. Sometimes the conditions will be marginal, but this is the moment to create rhythm from chop.

I often see people getting frustrated in the surf – perhaps moaning about the quality of the waves, the crowds, the 'wrong' tide, that they did not catch enough waves. This is reflected on land with a 'doing', not 'being', mode. You surely know the feeling: you cannot focus, running on autopilot, rushing. In the sea these feelings can evoke aggressive behaviour in people, especially through the phenomenon known as 'localism' (this is *my* break, you are an outsider). The slightest thing irritates (a missed wave, someone in 'your' way, a crowd). You feel threatened and your body tenses ready for action. We have all experienced this when we lash out physically or mentally (red mind).

We have to step out of negativity and reactive impulses, because this simply fosters the aggressive locals who are ready to fight and will not welcome even humble visitors. Perhaps you cannot stop this happening, but you can stop what happens next. Look away. Look around. Be aware of your mind. Be present and thus become content. Surfing should foster positivity, compassion, empathy (blue mind). Stand at the crest of the next wave and spread an infectious smile. Paddle up to visitors and say 'hi' – you will be amazed at how much a smiling hello can spread relaxation.

All surfers know the therapeutic feeling of waxing up before a surf. It perhaps fills your senses with the sweet smell of the ubiquitous Californian brand *SexWax*, sold in three-ounce plastic-wrapped bars: strawberry, pineapple, grape or coconut. Wax formulae have been treated as highly confidential trade secrets. Unfortunately, paraffin has been the main ingredient, with small amounts of beeswax added for pliability, Vaseline for lubrication and petrochemical resin for added stickiness. The ingredients are mixed and heated, then poured into metal moulds. Today, thankfully, there is a rainbow spectrum of eco-waxes, not dependent on petrochemicals.

It seems oh so simple, but one of the best ways to temper any sense of frustration or negativity you might have before a surf is to treat waxing your board as a meditation.

The process of waxing can start with a clean board or a waxed board needing extra beading for grip. A gentle circular motion is key. For every wax that you think of a negative – a wipeout, a wave missed – think of the opposite positive during the next wax motion: coming up safely for air, and the adrenalin of a fast paddle, respectively. This is about the duality of being and doing, the yin and the yang.

Continue this process with any thoughts that enter your mind while you wax. Follow preoccupation with the past or future by being in the present. Follow analysis with sensitivity. Follow depletion with nourishment. You can never have too much wax, so keep waxing until you bring your intentions, body and mind into alignment. *Being* is a place of choice and intention. This pure awareness allows you to surf with open senses, to know you are blessed to be alive.

Summary

Use the rhythmic process of waxing to eliminate frustration and negatives (red mind). When the *doing* of waxing has become *being*, paddle out, charged with the moment (blue mind). And following the surf, when the sun tips whole into the horizon, remember that the best bit can be afterwards. Stay present.

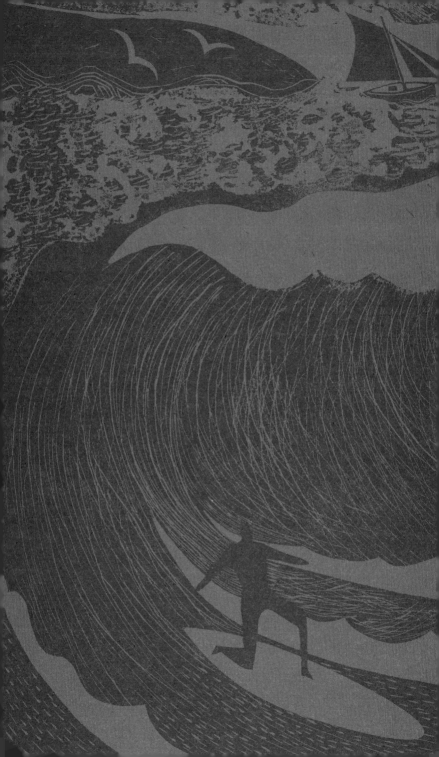

CHAPTER SEVEN

RIDING THE NEW WAVE

Surfing is not all at sea.
The future of wave-riding can satisfy inland
populations and could be part of health improvement
programmes within communities. We live in an age of
'governmentality', where even our own bodies are
regulated by outside influences — laws, directives and
prescriptions, many concerning diet and exercise. What
better than to bring surfing, an activity of bodily
fitness and mindfulness, to those who cannot access the
ocean through developing initiatives such as inland
wave pools, with their natural models
in river bores.

RIVER BORES & BLUE GYMS

◆

River bores are phenomenal sights to witness, but to experience surfing them provides a greater richness. First, they only happen every so often, so missing a wave means missing a year. Second, they seem to come out of nowhere.

WHEN THE OCEAN TIDE reaches the shallow water of a river (particularly pronounced at high and spring tides), if there is nothing in the river to impede or stop the tide (like a dam, or rapids) the crest can travel up the river creating a rideable wave, sometimes pronounced in size as the river narrows, the energy dissipating as the bottom friction of the river wears it down. Pioneered in the UK at the Severn Bore, river bore riding is now popular all over the world. The periodic tidal bore at the River Severn breaks twice a day on big incoming tides, most months of the year, for three to four days. The tides are largest around the spring and autumn equinoxes in March and September (coincidentally when my kids Ruben and Lola were born) and this is when most surfers ride the Severn.

Colonel Jack Churchill reputedly rode the bore prone on a wooden board in 1955. But a group of Newquay-based Australian lifeguards and surfboard shaper Bill Bailey were first witnessed riding the bore standing for almost a kilometre (about half a mile) in September 1962, against police advice

RIDING THE NEW WAVE

and the threat of arrest. Bore riding gained wider appeal when reigning British champion, Rodney Sumpter, rode it for an 'unofficial' 9.5 km (6 miles). Sections of this were filmed by his girlfriend, Simonne Renvoize, and edited into his first surf film *Come Surf With Me*, screened in 1967.

Rodney Sumpter chased bores up the Yangtze in China and the Bay of Fundy in Canada and surfed in the Congo for a 1968 *Surfer* magazine feature and television project. Bore riding is now a global challenge wherever the phenomenon occurs. French surfers frequently ride the Mascaret on the Dordogne river and Brazilians ride the Pororoca in the Amazon through crocodiles, snakes and piranhas. In 1988 Devon surfer Stuart Matthews and a support team surfed the bore breaking down the Qiantang River in China as part of a TV documentary. The film only included a short riding sequence on a 3-metre (10-foot) wave – disaster struck and the safety boat was capsized. Everyone survived, but valuable camera equipment was lost containing the best footage. Today there is an annual event on the 'Silver Dragon'.

A Marriage of Blue & Green

River surfing is perhaps the perfect marriage of the blue and green gyms. These movements have been spearheaded in the UK's National Health Service to promote health and well-being and appreciation of the countryside, coastline and inland waterways. This offers a way of saving millions of pounds where immersion in nature is a great prescription for physical and mental symptoms as an alternative to costly drug therapies, such as antidepressants. Regular contact with the natural environment has been proven to reduce stress, boost physical activity, create stronger communities and foster an increased awareness of the value of the natural environment. The catch, of course, is that the more we realize how important staying in touch with a 'clean' environment is, the more we seem bent on polluting that environment. Notice how many people jog with a plastic bottle of water. We must become more mindful of these contradictions.

River bores are the first step towards bringing surfing to people who do not live on the coast. The full transition is realized in the development of wave gardens and surfing lakes.

ENGINEERING PERFECTION

Surfers talk of 'mechanical' waves, craving the perfection of breaks such as Malibu in California, which on a good day unfolds with precision to produce long, almost identical rides. Imagine having the guarantee of perfect waves on your doorstep.

ONE OF THE MOST EXCITING ELEMENTS in the future of surfing is the development of inland surfing lakes and wave gardens. These can mimic orbital ocean waves, such as the *Surf Pool* designed by American company *Wave Loch* from

San Diego, or use the bow wave principle perfected at the *Wavegarden* testing facility in San Sebastian, Spain. The bow wave principle uses a machine (encased in a cage, underneath a pontoon) moving down a lake, creating a rideable wave either side of the pontoon. The bathymetry (bottom shape) of the lake can allow a number of rideable waves for varying abilities from one bow movement.

The Spain site is not open to the public, but is the home of a team developing the concept in order to sell the technology (with necessary installation, safety and management systems in place). Occasionally, it is opened for promotional and research purposes. The lake is set in a stunning river valley that protects it from the wind, but also limits the potential size of the wave. You wait for your ride sitting close to the pon-

The secret is to paddle towards the pontoon and take off

toon, the machine starts to move, instantly creating a bulge, and you start paddling. An immediate slight refraction in the wave bow causes a small current to pull you away from the pontoon, but the secret is to paddle towards the pontoon and take off. Once you are up and riding, it is similar to surfing a river bore. The big difference (aside from the contrast in catching the wave) is that in the ocean the power moves out from the curl of the wave towards the face, whereas a bow wave has maximum energy on the face, refracting away into the curl. The whitewater thus surges like a river bore.

While surfers pine for pointbreaks with long, almost identical rides, they also love the unpredictability of wildly changing beach break conditions. Most ocean surf is not 'perfect', even when combed by an offshore wind that helps to create a consistently peeling wave. Surfing my local break is often about making beauty from chaos, creating rhythm from disharmony. How can this paradox be addressed?

Sustainable Surfing

The latest advances in wave-making technology have been a source of inspiration for a *Wavegarden* recently opened in Snowdonia, Wales, and *The Wave UK* project, launched in Bristol using the *Wave Pool* design pioneered by Thomas Lochtefeld at *Wave Loch* in San Diego. Rather than raising water and dropping it into a sluice to produce a wave, *The Wave UK* system will use pneumatics (powered by renewable energy) to create radical pressure changes in the water (mimicking the impact of wind), causing circular wave motion to propagate across the lake, the breaking point and shape of which is then dictated by the local bathymetry. Eight waves per minute can be created, peeling across a number of zones to allow six people riding each wave. The technology also gives the ability to easily change the height and shape and power of the wave for varying surf standards. The diversity of wave shapes is key, addressing the paradox of the monotonous machine-like wave. Importantly, there are no working or moving parts in

the water, meaning no permanent structures inside the lake itself. Surfers can thus paddle back to the take-off zone, keep warm and get the strength they need to be able to transfer skills to the ocean environment.

TheWave UK is the unique vision of Nick Hounsfield, founder and CEO, who was deeply driven by the loss of his father in 2010 to make a big difference through a project that set out not only to improve the health of communities but to be a hallmark for creativity, sustainability and social impact. Of course, surfing is a driving force (and what a great driving force to have), but the vision is so much wider, creating both a green and blue gym that enriches every visitor through education and perhaps rehabilitation connected to the simple thrill of riding beautiful long peeling waves in a safe, accessible and democratic environment.

Nick Hounsfield explains: 'We want our project to be fun, thoughtful and engaging, yet have a big heart, serious thinking and a sustainable outlook. The more you educate yourselves about the issues facing this ecosystem, the more you'll want to help ensure its health – then share that knowledge to educate and inspire others.' Fusing nature and surfing is at the heart of *The Wave* UK. The site will offer a tremendous interaction with green space. Also, it will be a beacon for ethical trade, transport management, local food sourcing and green energy, reducing carbon footprints and using fewer plastics. And local universities are also on board to use the site as a

A Bright Future

I forecast that the positive outcomes from the new wave of surfing sites will range from high-level training for professional surfers, new events that showcase longboarding as dance choreographed to music, to empowerment programmes that improve the confidence and happiness of thousands of individuals, both young and old. Projects have sprung up around the UK to utilize surfing therapeutically with physically and mentally challenged persons and with those suffering from mental health problems, including post-traumatic stress disorder often suffered by ex-servicemen who have seen war duty. However, ocean surfing can be unpredictable – conditions can be too rough or there may be a flat spell with no swell. Wave sites provide a great environment for these kinds of therapeutic applications for surfing and for introducing mindfulness into such activities.

tsunami testing facility as part of both a humanitarian project and a campaign to inspire more girls to study engineering and science. Again, access to the beach and overcrowding can be a barrier for riding waves to many groups in society. This project leapfrogs those limitations by offering equal access to all in a sensibly managed location. The future of surfing has to fuse sustainability, education and ecology.

Olympic Performance

For every professional surfer, there are thousands more just surfing for fun, far removed from the hustle and bustle of contests. So-called 'free surfing' is true surfing for most. But the ancient Greeks developed competitive sport as a complex cultural and ritual occasion, birthing the Olympic Games. Competition remains an important element of surf culture. The International Surfing Association (ISA) has been pushing for surfing to be included as an Olympic sport for decades. Duke Kahanamoku advocated surfing as an Olympic sport in the early 1900s. In fact, the Sydney 2000 Olympics was very close to including surfing as a 'special sport'. There was also a surfing exhibition at the Melbourne Olympics in 1956. The ISA recently ran the first ever World Adaptive Surfing Championship for more physically challenged surfers. I have competed in what is dubbed the 'Olympics of Surfing' (the ISA World Surfing Games) and I firmly believe it will be fantastic for surfing to become a Paralympic Sport. Newsflash: it has been shortlisted for inclusion in Tokyo 2020. Watch this space.

The biggest challenge is having contestable surfing conditions close to the Olympic sites and developing an original format that captures the attention of the audience and the flair of surfing as performance. Perhaps wave sites can facilitate the relationship between surfing and music, where surfers perform to a soundtrack of their choice and are judged on style, interpretation, technical ability and flow.

Surfing the new wave of inland facilities should not be about heroic accounts of conquering and claiming, but a democratic wave open to all and potentially accessible by all, so the beginner and the expert alike can share the same buzz without the barriers of big egos and aggressive localism.

GUARDIANS OF THE OCEAN

There is nothing better to shock the system into the realities of the devastation of the planet than awe in the face of a sublime natural feature, recognizing forces greater than the human. Education through ecological perception and bodymindfulness is key.

SURF TRAVEL HAS AFFORDED ME the opportunity to experience some of the most inspiring landscapes and cultures on the planet. But as I return to these coastscapes I am witnessing the increasing impact of marine litter, crippling local communities. It is easy for our optimism for an ecologically sound future to be crushed when we visit places that are slowly choked by accumulating plastics, human effluent and metals leaching into the water. On so many occasions the locals are simply beyond doing anything about this, exhausted for ideas, exhausted by outsiders' suggestions.

In 2004 oceanographers at the University of Plymouth reported that small plastic pellets, known as mermaids' tears, had spread across all of the world's oceans. Ultimately these

are ingested by marine animals and zooplankton, bringing toxicity into the food chain. Surfers Against Sewage (SAS) highlighted the problem of mermaids' tears on UK beaches to the British Plastic Federation (BPF) in 2007, delivering a bottle of 10,000 mermaids' tears collected from one Cornish beach. Since then, SAS and the BPF have worked together on the Operation Clean Sweep (OCS) manual – aimed at changing factory practice, improving plastic factories' efficient use of plastic pellets and ridding the UK's coastline of mermaids' tears.

Global plastic consumption in 2016 is estimated to be 300 million tons. The decomposition rate of most plastic debris is horrifying: 450 years for a plastic bottle and 600 years for a fishing line. The ultimate symbol of our throwaway lifestyle is the plastic bag: over 500 billion are consumed annually – a million a minute. A culture of behavioural changes needs to blossom and be implemented at all levels. It starts with individual choices. This power resides within each and every one of us to reduce plastic consumption, participate in beach cleans and join environmental action groups like Surfers Against Sewage.

We also need to support and further explore eco-friendly green technologies in surfboard production because we are still heavily dependent upon petrochemical-based equipment – fibreglass and polyurethane, neoprene wetsuits, and urethane products. We should be world leaders in sustainable equipment, vital for the new generation.

Cultural Exchange

Green travel is not an option for the future but a necessity. If travel is part of your lifeblood, how do you square this with its negative environmental impact? There are no easy answers, yet travel should not be seen as escapism, but as a grounded and positive way to flag up and challenge our pressing global environmental concerns and facilitate cultural exchange. And eco-tourism needs to be allied with education, so schoolchildren learn about sustainability.

Despite my mixed feelings about my passion and dependence on travel, what really inspires me are the emerging surf cultures of Africa, Asia and the Caribbean. These are the communities that can add new flavour to surfing and crack its legacy of North American-centric and Australian-centric interests. Also, travel can take you deeply into ecological issues where it generates stark cultural comparisons, showing that consumerist capitalism is not the only or best measure of cultural development. Besides human cultural comparisons, the spirit of travelling with a conscience will bring you closer to the personalities of majestic landscapes as Other.

It Takes a Bit of Grit to Make a Pearl

As a surfer who travels a lot, I have flight time on my conscience. I advocate avoiding short-haul flights, flying direct, flying economy, choosing airlines with modern fleets and high capacity, avoiding night flights, avoiding winter flights, flying

less, staying longer and keeping luggage to a minimum. Importantly, recognition of the problem is part of the solution, where travellers face up to responsibility and do not ignore their carbon footprint. I think positive relationships with your local surf break are very important to foster as well. Local surfers are often the stewards of that coastline, the first to taste pollution in the water, to challenge poorly planned coastal developments. I hope that more surfers become political voices both locally and globally. A surfing world leader would be very exciting.

Yet are we also in danger of turning green values into a form of neo-imperialism, focusing upon reducing our carbon footprint but withdrawing a source of income from others through denial of eco-tourism, where we turn back to holidays at home while continuing to conspicuously consume energy? I have seen on my travels that sensitive cultural tourism can bring employment and resources to previously unstable and economically deprived corners of the world, such as Madagascar, the Philippines and Algeria. We are in a deep ecological crisis and none of us wants to pass on this dreadful legacy to future generations. It takes a bit of grit to make a pearl, but we must approach environmental challenges with resolution and desire. By reducing, reusing, recycling and travelling smart, we might continue to have the choice to live, surf and travel in clean, colourful, unpolluted places and to share that choice with others across the world.

SALTWATER SOUL

◆

Where other people have a hearth, I have a surfboard rack — climbing a wall in the high-roofed kitchen that overlooks the turbulent Atlantic Ocean with the next stop Halifax, Novia Scotia. This hearth warms me in ways only surfers can explain.

A LL OF THESE SURFBOARDS have been performance-tested in the giant tubs where the earth's floor dips away and oceans stretch their muscles in permanent salt-soak, testing my spirits as a saltwater scientist. Through surfing I have developed a range of meditations for my saltwater soul. My surfboards have been my magic carpets, taking me on journeys that can be retold in political, aesthetic and cultural terms. They have connected me with otherwise puzzling places, building bridges, learning civility and tolerance for others. They have provided a medium to transcend language and age barriers. There is nothing more satisfying than seeing local kids in Haiti having fun trying surfing for the first time and returning years later to see these kids hooked on surfing.

A Gift of the Present

In surfing, I have shaped an identity, forged a career. The surfboard for me is a ritual object, a totem. Most of the boards are custom made and then full of character — wooden stringers affording an umbilicus to the very birth of surfing in placental

Hawaii. Shapers' spirits have flowed through their hands into the blanks to give these longboards a talismanic presence.

The surfboard is a medium that allows you to translate the energy of the moving wave into an experience felt so deeply in your body, mind and spirit that you sing out, regardless of the wipeouts. The surfboard is more than a vehicle – it is inspired, as solid air, and flexible too: somewhere between fish and bird, whale and dolphin. It is the horizontal ladder to a limbo world, where, in traditional shamanic terms, you take out your skeleton, clean it, and put it back as you are rinsed over and over by rolling foam, or, on a good day, slip into an overhead tube where time stands still and the green world slides by as canopy and a thinking cap. Everyone has the right to surf. For me it is the ultimate meditation for a saltwater soul, a lesson in bodymindfulness, a gift of the present. Waves, surfing and surfers continue to inspire me, as they now do for my daughter Lola, who recently said: 'Dad, I want to surf with you in places I've never heard of.'

Till my soul is full of longing

For the secret of the sea,

And the heart of the great ocean

Sends a thrilling pulse through me.

FROM 'THE SECRET OF THE SEA'
HENRY WADSWORTH LONGFELLOW, AMERICAN POET, 1807–82

FURTHER READING

Bachelard, Gaston *Water and Dreams: An Essay on the Imagination of Matter* (Dallas Institute of Humanities & Culture, Dallas, 1983/1994)

Campbell, Joseph *The Power of Myth* (Bantam Doubleday Dell Publishing Group, New York, 1989)

Clark, Andy *Supersizing the Mind: Embodiment, Action, and Cognitive Extension* (Oxford University Press, Oxford, 2010)

Coleridge, Samuel Taylor *The Rime of the Ancient Mariner* (Folio Society, London, 1798/1994)

Davis, Wade *The Serpent and the Rainbow* (Pocket Books, New York, 1985)

Dass, B.R. Ram *Be Here Now* (Lama Foundation, San Cristobal, New Mexico, 1971)

De Landa, Manuel *A Thousand Years of Nonlinear History* (Zone Books, Cambridge, MA, 2000)

Deren, Maya *Divine Horsemen: The Living Gods of Haiti* (Thames and Hudson, London, 1953)

Derrida, Jacques *Writing and Difference* (Routledge, London, 1990)

Duane, Daniel *Caught inside: A Surfer's Year on the California Coast* (North Point Press, New York, 1997)

Dubois, Laurent *Haiti: The Aftershocks of History* (Metropolitan Books, New York, 2011)

Ford, Nicholas J. and Brown, David *Surfing and Social Theory: Experience, Embodiment and Narrative of the Dream Glide* (Routledge, London, 2006)

Gibson, James J. *The Ecological Approach to Visual Perception* (Houghton Mifflin, Boston, MA, 1979)

Goffman, Erving *The Presentation of Self in Everyday Life* (Doubleday, New York, 1959)

Harper, W. & Wallace, J. (eds), *Xenophon's Anabasis* (Harper & Brothers, New York, 1893)

Heidigger, Martin *Being and Time* (Wiley-Blackwell, Hoboken, 1927/1978)

Hemingway, Ernest *The Old Man and the Sea* (Arrow, Potomac, MD, 1951/1994)

Hillman, James *Re-Visioning Psychology* (HarperCollins, New York, 1992)

Hiss, Tony *In Motion: The Experience of Travel* (Alfred Knopf, New York, 2010)

Holmes, Paul *Dale Velzy is Hawk* (The Croul Family Foundation, Irvine, CA, 2006)

Jullien, François *A Treatise on Efficacy: Between Western and Chinese Thinking* (University of Hawaii Press, Honolulu, 2004)

Kapu'sci'nski, Ryszard *Another Day of Life* (Penguin, London, 1976/2001)

Kapu'sci'nski, Ryszard *The Other* (Verso Books, London, 2008)

Kerouac, Jack *On The Road* (Penguin, London, 1957/2000)

Kotler, Steven *West of Jesus: Science, Surfing, and the Origins of Belief* (Bloomsbury, New York, 2007)

Lingis, Alphonso *Abuses* (University of California Press, Berkeley, CA, 1994/95)

Lingis, Alphonso *Dangerous Emotions* (University of California Press, Berkeley, CA, 1999/2000)

Lingis, Alphonso *Trust* (University of Minnesota Press, Minneapolis, 2004)

Lingis, Alphonso *Violence and Splendor* (Northwestern University Press, Evanston, IL, 2011)

Lippard, Lucy R. *The Lure of the Local: Senses of Place in a Multicentred Society* (The New Press, New York, 1997)

Livingstone, David N. *The Geographical Tradition* (Blackwell, Oxford, 1993)

London, Jack *The Call of the Wild* (William Collins, London, 1903/2011)

Martin, Andy *Walking on Water* (Minerva, New York, 1992)

Martin, Andy *Stealing the Wave: The Epic Struggle Between Ken Bradshaw and Mark Foo* (Bloomsbury, New York, 2008)

Massey, Doreen B. *For Space* (Sage, London, 2005)

Melville, Herman *Moby-Dick* (Folio Society, London, 1851/2009)

Morgan, Bill *Selected Letters of Allen Ginsberg and Gary Snyder 1956–1991* (Counterpoint, New York, 2009)

Nichols, Wallace J. *Blue Mind: The Surprising Science That Shows How Being Near, In, On, or Under Water Can Make You Happier, Healthier, More Connected, and Better at What You Do* (Little, Brown, London, 2014)

Nietzsche, Friedrich *Beyond Good and Evil* (Penguin, London, 1886/2003)

Padel, Ruth *In and Out of the Greek Mind: Greek Images of the Tragic Self* (Princeton University Press, Princeton, NJ, 1992)

Perse, Saint-John *Anabasis* (Mariner Books, New York, 1924/1970)

Pirsig, Robert *Zen and the Art of Motorcycle Maintenance* (William Morrow and Company, New York, 1974)

Redgrove, Peter *Selected Poems* (Jonathan Cape, London, 1999)

Rimbaud, Arthur *Complete Works, Selected Letters* (The University of Chicago Press, Chicago, 1871/2005)

Sartre, Jean-Paul *Being and Nothingness: An Essay on Phenomenological Ontology* (Routledge Classics, London, 1943/2003)

Schön, Donald A. *The Reflective Turn: Case Studies In and On Educational Practice* (Teachers Press, Columbia University, New York, 1991)

Self, Will *Psychogeography* (Bloomsbury Publishing, London, 2007)

Sinclair, Iain *London Orbital* (Goldmark, London, 2002)

Stevens, Wallace *Harmonium* (Faber & Faber, London, 1923/2001)

Tarnas, Richard *The Passion of the Western Mind: Understanding the Ideas That Have Shaped Our World View* (Pimlico, London, 2010)

Taussig, Michael *What Colour is the Sacred?* (Cambridge University Press, Cambridge, 2009)

Warshaw, Matt *The History of Surfing* (Chronicle Books, San Francisco, 2013)

Weisbecker, Allan C. *In Search of Captain Zero: A Surfer's Road Trip Beyond the End of the Road* (Tarcher, New York, 2001)

Winton, Tim *Breath* (Picador, Oxford, 2008)

Young, Nat *The Complete History of Surfing: From Water to Snow* (Allen & Unwin, Crows Nest, NSW, 2008)

INDEX

DEDICATION

For Mum and Dad
— Susan and Alan — the most
brilliantly creative and inspiring
people I know. Thank you for teaching
me to follow my heart and to explore
and experience the cultural and
physical wonders of the world; from
literature to landscapes to
art to words to waves.

MINDFULNESS AND SURFING

DEDICATION

*For Mum and Dad
— Susan and Alan — the most
brilliantly creative and inspiring
people I know. Thank you for teaching
me to follow my heart and to explore
and experience the cultural and
physical wonders of the world; from
literature to landscapes to
art to words to waves.*